MY
HEART
HURTS

Finding Hope in Heartache

CINDY HOBBS JANECKA

cj books

CJ Books may be ordered through booksellers or by visiting www.cindyjanecka.com.

Certain stock imagery © Thinkstock.

ISBN: 978-1-943092-24-6 (sc)
ISBN: 978-1-943091-02-7 (hc)
ISBN: 978-1-943091-79-9 (e)

Printed in the United States of America

CJ Books rev. date 03/13/2018

Dad,
Your love, leadership and faith have
greatly impacted my life and continue
to be the cornerstone of our family.
I am so grateful you are my dad
and especially thankful you are my friend.

Contents

Acknowledgements

My heart is filled with love and gratitude as I am reminded of the many friends and family—and even those we had never met—who lifted up Mom and our family in their prayers during this incredibly difficult journey. We have experienced what it means to "share one another's burdens" because you helped to bear some of the seemingly unbearable weight of our heartbrokenness. Each of you who loved and cared for us during that time were a vivid expression of God's mercy, grace and provision in our lives, and your warm and heartfelt memories and stories of Mom continue to bless our family.

To Mom's loving family and friends—Thank you for your prayers and support throughout this unimaginable journey. Each of you knows how special you were to Mom and the place you held in her heart, and it is my hope that sharing this story will bring you peace and comfort to know that her faith and trust in God was unwavering.

Sherrie Sheets, RN—The care and compassion you showed for Mom brought our family great comfort. I am so grateful that God placed you in our lives—and especially in Mom's—in what has been our darkest hour and time of greatest need.

Dr. Matthew Davis and Dr. David Ciceri—Although your lives are filled with caring for an abundance of patients, your care for Mom and the compassion and leadership you demonstrated to our family will never be forgotten and are deeply appreciated.

Dr. Kazim Sheikh—Thank you for your willingness to come see Mom and our family. God used you and your compassion, sincerity, expertise, and honesty to lead us to the difficult answers we had been earnestly seeking.

Dr. Keith Horner—Your ministry far exceeds your services as a medical provider. Our family greatly appreciates your wisdom, compassion and faith. Thank you for helping us navigate another difficult medical journey.

Larry, Terri Kay, Angie, and Andy—Our family has traveled down many difficult paths and through troubled times, and God continues to use each of our strengths and gifts to love, care for and support each other in our times of greatest need. I am thankful for each of you, and I love you.

Carey, Colby and Courtney—The pages of this book are filled with the lessons that God has taught me throughout my life. I know it would be Grandma's prayer, as it is my own, that these truths would be written upon your hearts to prepare you for your own trials and adversities in life. I love you deeply.

Darrell—You once again journeyed alongside me through one of the deepest valleys I have yet traveled, and I am incredibly grateful for your unwavering love and devotion. Throughout each of our family's trials, you continue to serve and care for us in ways that no one else is able to do. I love your servant's heart. You truly are the love of my life.

Brenda Kay Keeton Hobbs—Mom, you committed your life to encouraging others in the midst of heartache, and my prayer is that the words in this book will continue to proclaim that message of hope through Jesus Christ and that God will be glorified!

Introduction

Life is filled with joyous occasions and countless blessings, but it is also filled with times of relentless despair and intense suffering. In a matter of hours, we can move from celebrating the birth of a child to memorializing the life of a loved one. Broken relationships and hurting families, health problems and debilitating diseases, natural disasters and those created by human hands, injustices and the ravages of war—and so many more adversities we face in life—can lead us to a deep longing for relief from the pain and suffering that accompany them.

The emotions experienced throughout life are in constant fluctuation, but the God of this life is never-changing. When life is uncertain, God is unwaveringly steady. These are not lofty words by someone who is not familiar with heartache and grief. Instead, my life has been filled with both. As exhilarating as life has been, at times, it has also been devastating and excruciatingly painful.

On a beautiful fall day in October, a journey began of what was to become one of the most difficult experiences of my life. What started as a normal day in the life of my family, ended with my mom in a debilitating and perplexing condition. In just a matter of hours, she went from being a vibrant and life-filled mother, grandmother, wife and friend to a woman trapped in a motionless body, unable to move or speak.

The lessons my mom taught me and the impact she has had on my life could fill volumes, but the words in this book are not intended to focus on myself or even on my mom's story. Instead, they are written to paint a picture of the strength and hope that God provides for each of us in all circumstances. Through a personal relationship with God through the saving grace of Jesus Christ, we are able to experience His immeasurable comfort and peace during the difficult and trying times of our lives.

At the beginning of each chapter are excerpts from some of Mom's favorite hymns. As for so many people, hymns were an important part of the foundation of her faith. Since she was young, the power of God's Word and truths set to music provided her great comfort and life-giving strength. She loved to sit at her piano and play and sing hymns—sometimes filled with joy and sometimes wrought with pain. During Mom's time in the hospital, she listened to hymns every day. When her blood pressure would rise or the pain would intensify, she would request to listen to her beloved hymns. The words which ministered to her for so many years became some of the greatest sources of comfort throughout her darkest days.

Each chapter also contains excerpts from the journals our family kept. Some of them are from the CaringBridge website entries which we shared with family and friends who were so desperately seeking information and direction on how to pray for us. Other entries are from my own journal of Mom's journey.

Like so many others who have encountered heartbreaking circumstances in life, I often felt unprepared and ill-equipped to face the devastation of my mom's illness. I experienced confusion, fear and exhaustion, but I also experienced God's grace, hope and extraordinary love. When the doubt of life began to swallow me up in its dark abyss, God's light would shine deeply into my heart. When I was unable to understand or comprehend our circumstances, God reminded me He is all-knowing and has complete clarity. When I felt I couldn't continue on, God lifted me up in His loving arms and carried me. This is a story of a 60-day journey of heartache and hope, a story of suffering and trusting, and how my mom taught me the greatest lesson of all.

Leaning on the Everlasting Arms

What a fellowship, what a joy divine,
Leaning on the everlasting arms!
What a blessedness, what a peace is mine,
Leaning on the everlasting arms!

Leaning, leaning,
Safe and secure from all alarms;
Leaning, leaning,
Leaning on the everlasting arms.

The eternal God is your refuge,
and underneath are the everlasting arms.

Deuteronomy 33:27

1 "This is it."

Day 1 – Saturday - 11:30 am

Last night Mom began to experience numbness in her hands and feet. By early this morning, she was unable to stand or use her hands. Although she has feeling in these areas, she also feels paralyzed and unable to control them. At 6 am she was taken by ambulance to the emergency room. She has had a CT scan and ruled out a stroke, and the MRI of her spine was clear. The doctors will admit her to the ICU and work with a neurologist to find a diagnosis. She is, of course, very scared and uncertain of what all this means, especially since her symptoms continue to worsen. Please pray for her, for my dad, and for our family. Please pray for doctors to have wisdom in their diagnosis and treatment of her.

With love and appreciation,
Brenda's Family

So do not fear, for I am with you; do not be dismayed,
for I am your God. I will strengthen you and help you;
I will uphold you with my righteous right hand.

Isaiah 41:10

Mom's first symptoms had actually begun two nights earlier. Thursday night Mom was unable to sleep and experienced horrible pain all over her body. She said the pain was especially intense in her legs and lower back. She cried throughout the night, and in the early hours of Friday morning, she asked Dad to take her to the emergency room. After being evaluated and undergoing various tests, the doctors said that their best guess as to the source of the pain was a negative interaction of the drugs she had been taking—an anti-inflammatory for her knee and an over-the-counter cold medicine. They injected her with a large dose of morphine, provided her with a prescription for Vicodin, and sent her home.

As Mom was preparing to be discharged from the emergency room, I happened to be at the office of our family physician who was also Mom's doctor. When I described Mom's pain and the hospital's response and lack of diagnosis, the doctor expressed his concern that she could be suffering from a rare condition called "Guillain-Barré Syndrome." As I walked out of our physician's office, I called Dad to express the doctor's concerns that Mom might have some rare condition that "I can't remember the name of." I recall Dad's voice and how concerned he sounded—which was very unusual.

My sister and I decided to spend Friday night at Mom and Dad's house, concerned about her condition. Mom sat up in her bed that evening with a perplexed look on her face. She kept flicking her fingertips and commenting on what an odd sensation she was experiencing and how her fingers felt slightly numb. Her symptoms seemed different from those she had experienced the previous night. There was now more numbness than pain.

At 5 am Saturday morning, Dad came upstairs and calmly said, "We have a problem with Mom." Those were his exact words. He said he heard her crying in the morning darkness and didn't know where she was because she was not in bed next to him. He then realized she was on the floor unable to walk due to the severe weakness in her legs. By the time he came upstairs that morning to tell us, he had helped her into a rolling desk chair and called an ambulance. When we came downstairs, Mom was very dismayed at her condition but also very adamant that she did not want to be taken back to the hospital. As we waited for the ambulance by the front door, she said to me: "Have them take me to the nursing home. I don't need to go to the hospital. This is it. It's over. I'm not coming home." I attempted to reassure her and tell her that she was overreacting and that the doctors could help her, but she would not waver in her objections. She knew.

> *God is in every tomorrow,*
> *Therefore I live for today.*
> *Certain of finding at sunrise,*
> *Guidance and strength for my way;*
> *Power for each moment of weakness,*
> *Hope for each moment of pain,*
> *Comfort for every sorrow,*
> *Sunshine and joy after the rain.*[1]

Several years ago, my ten-year old son was preparing to attend a new school. I was anxious because he only knew a few kids in the school, and we had been praying together for months for God to prepare him for the new friendships and experiences that were before him. The night before school began, we were talking about the next day, and he spoke amazing words of faith and wisdom: "Mom, I don't have to worry about tomorrow. God is already there."

Even though we didn't understand what was happening to Mom at the time, we didn't need to be afraid. God was already there. Even when the doctors were unable to explain Mom's condition, God knew. Even when they didn't know what the prognosis would be, God knew. Even when we were unable to fully comprehend what was to come, God knew. Not only did He know, but He had also prepared us for everything we would need to help us through the days ahead. He was already there.

"I am the Alpha and the Omega," says the Lord God,
"who is, and who was, and who is to come, the Almighty."
Revelation 1:8

God is the Alpha and the Omega. He is the beginning and the end. He transcends time. He is all-knowing, all-powerful and all-present. When we are in circumstances that are painful or experience the fear of the unknown or unthinkable, we can rest in the assurance that God will never leave us. He is with us as we make important decisions. He is with us when we are unable to control our tears and are overcome with grief and sadness. He is there when we rejoice and celebrate, and He is there when we feel that we are unable to walk another step on a treacherous and painful journey. When we feel we can't go on, God's everlasting arms will pick us up and carry us. He knows what lies before us, and His provision is, and always will be, sufficient. There is great comfort in acknowledging God's sovereignty and knowing that He is already there. And when I am reminded of that truth, I am able to find a peace that truly does transcend my own understanding [Philippians 4:7].

"This is it." Those were the words Mom spoke to me early that morning as we waited on the ambulance to arrive. Somehow she knew. God had prepared her. We didn't know, but she knew—and God knew.

Be strong and courageous.
Do not be afraid or terrified because of them,
for the Lord your God goes with you;
he will never leave you nor forsake you.

Deuteronomy 31:6

It Is Well

When peace, like a river, attendeth my way,
When sorrows like sea billows roll;
Whatever my lot, Thou has taught me to say,
It is well, it is well, with my soul.

It is well, with my soul,
It is well, with my soul,
It is well, it is well, with my soul.

Run now, I pray thee, to meet her, and say unto her,
"Is it well with thee? Is it well with thy husband?
Is it well with the child?" And she answered, "It is well."

2 Kings 4:26 KJV

2 A Ton of Bricks

Day 1 – Saturday - 9:00 pm

The paralysis has progressed to the point that Mom is unable to move from her neck down. She has been diagnosed with Guillain-Barré Syndrome—a condition that attacks the nervous system and causes paralysis. She basically became paralyzed from the neck down over a 12-hour period. She was admitted to the medical intensive care unit, and the decision was made to put her on life support to help her breathe, since her lungs were becoming impacted as well. The doctors also said that she needed to be put in a medically induced coma for a period of time that could range from one week to several months. We all had a chance to talk to her before she was sedated. Mom is an incredibly strong woman with a deep faith. She was fully aware of the decision and the treatment. Although there is so much we are unsure of at this time, we have to hold on to that which we are certain: God's love for Mom is more than all of our love combined, and she has instilled in us the strength and faith we will need to get through this. We trust God with her health and her life.

Be joyful in hope, patient in affliction, faithful in prayer.

Romans 12:12

Throughout the day doctors ordered various tests, blood work, scans, and procedures that might provide some clarity on Mom's diagnosis. As the hours went by, we helplessly watched the illness progress, and she complained that she hurt all over and was never able to find a comfortable position. When she first arrived at the hospital, she was able to lift her legs as she lay on the bed, and she had full movement of her upper body. But by early afternoon, she was no longer able to move her legs at all, and eventually needed assistance to move her arms. The doctor asked her to touch her nose with her finger, and she was unable to do so. By 6 pm, she was barely able to shrug her shoulders.

A pulmonologist from a nearby hospital came and talked to us and explained Guillain-Barré Syndrome (GBS), how the paralysis progresses and how it should eventually reverse. The doctor said it would take months to recover, but that she was certain Mom would be able to do so. She was at risk of losing the ability to breathe on her own because the paralysis was moving upward in her body so quickly, so the team of doctors wanted to put her in a medically induced coma and place her on a ventilator until the disease began to reverse. There were only two treatments for GBS—both of which could possibly stop the progression: IVIg injections and a plasma exchange procedure called plasmapheresis. They wanted to begin the IVIg injections immediately and would later re-evaluate to see if the plasma exchange procedure was warranted.

All of this was explained in Mom's presence, and she agreed to the recommended treatment and procedures. It was 7 pm. Mom spoke to each of us with confidence and assurance—not that she would recover—but that she knew what she wanted to say to each of us. Even though we kept telling her this was not "goodbye," she somehow knew that those would be the last words she would speak to us. Once she had finished addressing each of us, she calmly said, "Let's get on with it."

He will have no fear of bad news; his heart is steadfast,
trusting in the Lord. His heart is steady, he will not be afraid,
until he looks in triumph on his adversaries.

Psalm 112:7-8

When we had first learned about the rarity of Guillain-Barré Syndrome and that only 1 in 100,000 people suffer from it, Dad said calmly—but with certainty—that GBS would most likely be Mom's diagnosis. That's just how things usually turned out for our family. As all families do, we had faced our share of trials and struggles. Yet through the years, we had also faced an unusual amount of uniquely difficult and uncommon circumstances. A close friend made the same observation years earlier and asked me: "How do these things always happen to your family?" It was a very good question and something I often wondered myself. But we are also a family that has experienced an abundance of God's provision and grace. The immense blessings have always accompanied the intense trials.

God is the author of all the blessings and gifts in our lives, which we so eagerly receive, and it can be difficult for us to accept that He allows us to suffer as well. The hardships we face are not apart from God's abundant love for us. Instead, they produce in us the very perseverance, character and hope for which we are called to develop as children of God. He will never allow us to suffer without His limitless provision of strength and grace to sustain us.

But we also glory in our sufferings,
because we know that suffering produces perseverance;
perseverance, character; and character, hope.

Romans 5:3-4

Hardship or tragedy often takes us by surprise. We aren't usually expecting it. It comes in many forms and from all directions. The saying: "It hit me like a ton of bricks" is often quite accurate. That is what it can feel like—an unbearable weight that suddenly descends upon us. We often feel unprepared to face it, as it leaves destruction and dismay in its path. There are times in our lives that we are forced to make important and sometimes urgent decisions in the wake of such chaos, and we feel ill-equipped to do so. Due to our lack of knowledge and preparedness, we may struggle as we face difficult parenting decisions, navigate unforeseen changes in a relationship or career, face a daunting disease, or experience a sudden and tragic loss. Yet nothing takes God by surprise, and He allows nothing to overtake us that we are not equipped to handle. When we are helpless, He is all-powerful. When we feel unprepared, He is perfectly capable. When we have nothing to give, He is ready to give us everything we need. And He will never leave us.

The day Mom became paralyzed and was placed on life support, I could never have imagined what would unfold and the devastation to come in the days ahead. Although, at times, I felt ill-equipped and incapable of handling it, I was reminded of the countless promises throughout Scripture that say otherwise. God was with me. God had prepared me. God had prepared Mom. I believed this for myself and for my family, and I also believed it for my mom.

Even with all the advancements of modern medicine and medical treatment, with the information and research of the internet at our fingertips, and with an army of friends and family members praying and standing by to help—there was nothing to do and no way to stop the progression of this horrifying and debilitating disease. Nothing. Our only choice was to place our faith, our hope, our trust—and Mom—in the arms of God. So we did.

My God is my rock, in whom I take refuge,
my shield and the horn of my salvation.
He is my stronghold, my refuge and my savior.

2 Samuel 22:3

He Leadeth Me

He leadeth me, O blessed thought!
O words with heav'nly comfort fraught!
Whate'er I do, where'er I be
Still 'tis God's hand that leadeth me.

He leadeth me, He leadeth me,
By His own hand He leadeth me;
His faithful follower I would be,
For by His hand He leadeth me.

The Lord is my shepherd, I lack nothing. He makes me lie down
in green pastures, he leads me beside quiet waters.

Psalm 23:1-2

3 Hope in a Plan

Day 2 – Sunday - 9:15 am

Mom remains in a medically induced coma and on life support. She was stable throughout the night, and her breathing has stabilized on the ventilator. We are now making the necessary arrangements to transfer her to a different hospital as soon as possible. Please pray for peace, hope and strength for our family—especially for Dad.

We learned that a hospital two hours away was renowned for their ability to administer the plasmapheresis treatment, and we decided to take Mom there. We immediately began to make the necessary arrangements. We had a plan. We knew what the next step would be. We began systematically making the calls and arrangements necessary to transfer Mom: the care flight team and helicopter, preparing a team of doctors for her arrival at the new hospital, and making arrangements for our own lodging in order to be nearby. We discussed each of our work schedules, logistics with kids and spouses, and what needed to happen in order to best coordinate her care. Our family always worked best with a plan, and there was a sudden infusion of confidence and hope once we had developed a course of action. Just hours before, we had felt helpless, confused and frustrated—not knowing what to do. Now we were suddenly feeling more empowered because we had a plan.

The Lord Almighty has sworn, "Surely, as I have planned,
so it will be, and as I have purposed, so it will stand."
Isaiah 14:24

The different arrangements that had to align did so seamlessly in a matter of hours. God had prepared the place and the people for Mom's transfer and care. We felt very strongly that God was leading us in our decisions and in our plans, and we had already begun to witness how He was orchestrating our steps and our ways. Just as a plan gave us a renewed sense of hope and confidence, we can rest in the promise that God, too, always has a plan.

Every person has a journey to travel as they walk through life, and only God knows exactly where that journey will take each of us. That is why the journey requires faith—trusting God enough to go willingly on that journey regardless of the mountains we will encounter or the valleys into which we must descend. Having faith in the face of uncertainty can be challenging, and that which is unknown can be frightening. Yet because God loves us with an everlasting and unfathomable love, we can trust Him. When we are frightened and confused or crying out in anger or despair, there is a safety and security in trusting our all-knowing God who always has a plan for our lives and the lives of those we love.

...so that no one would be unsettled by these trials.
For you know quite well that we are destined for them.
1 Thessalonians

Throughout scripture God tells us that we will face many trials in our lives. Just as adversity is part of His plan for us, so is the confidence that He will be with us through it all, providing exactly what we need to endure our hardships and to be sustained. God is always present and always at work. He always reigns. God is always on His throne. When we cannot make sense of our circumstances, we can trust that God is able to do just that. When we don't have a plan, we can be assured that He has a meticulously calculated and perfect one in place. Sometimes He chooses to immediately give us a clear understanding of why something happens, and sometimes it might be days or years later before we gain that insight. And then there are the times we must wait until we get to Heaven to fully comprehend His plan and His purpose.

There is no circumstance, no trouble,
no testing, that can ever touch me until,
first of all, it has gone past God
and past Christ, right through to me.
If it has come that far,
it has come with a great purpose.[2]

At the time she became sick, Mom had been writing and leading a weekly Bible study for more than a decade. The last Bible study she led was just three days before becoming paralyzed. That day one of the ladies asked her how much longer she planned on teaching. Without hesitation, she confidently replied: "God will make it clear when it is time to stop." She believed with an unwavering faith and confidence that God had a plan and would reveal it when He was ready. And three days later, He did just that. Knowing that Mom trusted in God's plan for her life was a great comfort to me.

*A Christian's troubles advance God's
purposes, purposes only He can fully
understand. As a human, you try so
hard to understand. But if God could be
fully understood, where's the power and
sovereignty in that? What would make
Him any different than just another smart
human? He is above all; His ways are
so perfect that a mere human could not
possibly understand on this side of heaven.
This is why you can place your absolute
trust and your life in Him, despite the pain
and the heartache. Because He is the God
above all, when you get to heaven and see
the world from His point of view, you will
be astounded by the perfection
of His loving plan.[3]*

There is so much in life that is unpredictable. There are waves of pain that sweep over us when we least expect it and obstacles that appear in our paths that we had never imagined. Those are the times in which we can feel helpless, uncertain and overwhelmed. When Mom became sick, I had to believe that there was a purpose behind the chaos that suddenly descended upon us. Believing and trusting that God had a plan—even if it was going to be difficult and painful—provided the hope and security that I desperately needed.

When life feels unpredictable and out of my control, I have to rest upon the firm foundation of God's sovereignty, His love for me, and His promise that nothing happens apart from His plan for my life, which is always greater than my own.

*Now faith is being sure of what we hope for
and certain of what we do not see.*

Hebrews 11:1

I Love to Tell the Story

I love to tell the story of unseen things above,
Of Jesus and His glory, of Jesus and His love.
I love to tell the story, because I know 'tis true;
It satisfies my longings as nothing else can do.

I love to tell the story, 'twill be my theme in glory,
To tell the old, old story of Jesus and His love.

Come and hear, all you who fear God;
let me tell you what he has done for me.

Psalm 66:16

---

4 Seated at Her Table

Day 2 – Sunday - 7:00 pm

Mom was airlifted to a hospital several hours away. She has been admitted to the medical intensive care unit and is already experiencing amazing care. Within minutes of her arrival, she was settled in her room, had undergone blood work, been attended to by two nurses and had already seen the neurologist. We definitely feel that this is the right place for her, and that the care will be excellent. All of this is such an encouragement to us.

The doctors here explained that they were not going to keep Mom in a medically induced coma throughout the active phase of the illness. They said that they would work to find a balance between sufficiently managing her pain and keeping her alert enough to be able to evaluate any progress she might be making, as well as maintain the ability to assess any additional complications that may occur (problems with her heart, brain, etc.). They also recommended that we begin plasma exchange immediately, followed by the IVIg injections. A central line was placed in her neck for the plasma exchange procedure. Mom performed so poorly on the nerve conduction test that the doctor actually checked the equipment repeatedly to make sure it was working properly. He even tested it on himself and finally concluded that Mom's results were "profoundly abnormal."

We are certain that Mom can hear us and understand us, since she sometimes responds with expressions with her eyes when we talk to her.

GBS is an autoimmune disease in which the body begins to attack itself, destroying the insulation (myelin sheath) surrounding the axons (extensions of the nerve cells). In the most severe cases, the disease will continue to progress, and the body will eventually destroy the nerves themselves. As more tests were conducted and more doctors evaluated her, we learned that Mom was not only suffering from a condition that affects only 1 in 100,000 people, but that her condition was even rarer than that statistic. Mom was still unable to speak or move any part of her body except her eyes. However, her mind was clear, and she was fully aware of her circumstances and everything that was happening. Seeing her trapped inside her body with no way of expressing herself was heartbreaking. The condition that had suddenly overtaken Mom's body was unimaginable when considering what her life had been like just days before.

Share with the Lord's people who are in need.
Practice hospitality.
Romans 12:13

The best way to understand Mom would be to understand the life she lived and the lives she touched. She did not impact people by the thousands or even hundreds. She never wrote a book. She never spoke to an auditorium full of people. She did not make appearances on television or the radio. Instead, Mom impacted the people God placed in her life through her individual relationships with them. She had a special gift that allowed her to recognize the needs of others, to truly see into their hearts, and understand how to minister to them. The lives Mom touched were truly reached one by one.

Mom was often the life of the party—and usually hosting it. Her deep love for others and her ministry in their lives were evidenced by those who had been seated at her table through the years. The doors to her heart and home were always open. God had undoubtedly blessed her with the gift of hospitality, which manifested itself in an unceasing passion for having people in her home. Every guest who entered her house experienced a warm welcome, usually accompanied by a glass of her famous "sweet tea."

Even our meals at holidays were extended to family and friends who were alone, and she always made a place for them at her table. I have no recollection of a holiday meal that did not include those beyond our immediate family. It would not be unusual for her and Dad to host 40-60 people for Easter, Thanksgiving or Christmas, and she did so with joy and ease. Being with people infused her with energy, and she was always looking forward to planning or hosting the next gathering.

Cheerfully share your home with those who need a meal or a place to stay. God has given each of you a gift from his great variety of spiritual gifts. Use them well to serve one another.

1 Peter 4:9-10 NLT

Mom had a special love for the Christmas holidays. She began celebrating Christmas immediately after Thanksgiving lunch. She would sit at the piano playing and singing, "We Wish You a Merry Christmas," as others would roll the fully decorated Christmas tree out of her beloved "Christmas Tree Closet" and place it in front of the window. By the Monday after Thanksgiving, there were no more signs of Fall and cornucopias. Instead, every surface of her house was adorned with some form of Christmas. Then the holidays were filled with her gracious hosting of parties for the neighbors, Dad's company employees, groups from their church, members of various charities and organizations, and a host of family birthdays and traditions. Mom's gift of hospitality was one she cherished giving away. But Mom never allowed all of the hustle, bustle, gift-giving and hosting to overshadow the true meaning of the Christmas season—the celebration of the birth of her Savior, Jesus Christ, to whom she had committed her life.

The weekly Bible study Mom taught also took place around her dining room table. She wrote each lesson from inspirations she received from her Bible reading, a book she read, or perhaps a headline in the news. God continuously taught her and guided her in her writing and teaching, so that she could, in turn, share God's truths and lessons with those seated at her table each week.

But in your hearts revere Christ as Lord. Always be prepared to give an answer to everyone who asks you to give the reason for the hope that you have but do this with gentleness and respect.

1 Peter 3:15

Many of those who came to her home were seeking counsel and comfort in the midst of difficult circumstances they were facing in their lives. A significant part of Mom's ministry transpired in the one-on-one conversations she had with people she knew and also with those who were given her name by a mutual friend as someone who could offer encouragement and guidance. She was always willing to share the lessons she had learned from the tragedies and trials she had faced in her life if it would offer even a glimmer of hope to someone else. Mom's ministry to those God placed in her path was an outpouring of what He had done in her own life and family. Life had not been easy for Mom, yet she was always eager to share the ways God had helped her by supplying His grace, mercy and strength through the years of difficulties and struggles.

Mom never claimed to "have all the answers" and did not boast of some great gift of wisdom. Instead, she was very humble and willing to talk of the mistakes she felt she had made in parenting, marriage and life. Perhaps the reason people could relate to her so well and trust her enough to share their own struggles and heartache was because she was willing to discuss her own mistakes and talk about the areas in which she continued to struggle. She truly believed that God was using the adversities she had endured to help others who were facing difficulties in their own lives. Because of that, she had a private yet powerful ministry with countless hurting individuals. We had witnessed her love for her family and friends, yet we would learn in the years to come that there were so many more lives she touched and acts of kindness she performed, known only to those who received them.

And whatever you do, whether in word or deed,
do it all in the name of the Lord Jesus,
giving thanks to God the Father through him.
Colossians 3:17

Although people were amazed at Mom's ability to cook, host and entertain guests, what truly defined her was her faith in Jesus Christ. It permeated all she did and everything she believed. Her life was centered on the truths that God had written on her heart for more than 70 years. She impressed these truths upon the hearts of her children and grandchildren, she shared them with the ladies in her Bible study each week, and they were the foundation of her friendships and relationships with everyone she knew. The strength of her faith was apparent throughout her life—in times of joyous celebration and in times of utter tragedy. Like so many others, she wrestled with the difficult questions in life of why things would happen and how to get through them, but the answers always led her back to her faith and trust in God through Jesus Christ.

Just days earlier, Mom's life had been filled with an abundance of commitments and engagements, and written on her calendar were the many activities recently accomplished and also those yet to come. Yet now she lay there unable to move and hooked up to endless tubes and machines upon which her life depended. Everything changed so suddenly, so unexpectedly and so drastically.

We desperately wanted the nurses and doctors who cared for Mom to understand the person she had been just days before—and the person she still was. They could only see that motionless, silent patient in front of them, but her heart, mind and soul were still infused with the life-filled person that we knew her to be. We taped a large picture of her over the hospital bed and often talked of her personality, talents, gifts and love for others, so that those caring for her could get a glimpse of her beauty and vibrancy.

Charm is deceptive, and beauty does not last;
but a woman who fears the Lord will be greatly praised.
Reward her for all she has done.
Let her deeds publicly declare her praise.

Proverbs 30:30-31

There is often disbelief and confusion when tragedy befalls someone whom we feel "doesn't deserve it." Why would someone who has spent her entire life loving, serving and caring for others have to endure such suffering? Or why would God allow a young and innocent child to experience pain, sickness or even death? I have learned that the answers to these questions are not easily found. Instead of drowning in the confusion and perplexity of what I don't understand, I try to focus on that which I am certain: God is a God of unending hope and unwavering love. Even in the midst of my uncertainty and questions, I know that His will for my life is to trust in that hope and love and share it with the people He places in my path.

Mom's life was also filled with opportunities to share God's love and hope with others throughout a lifetime of trials. She knew that God had a plan and purpose in all that happened in her life and the lives of those she loved, and she trusted that He would provide what she needed to get through another day and another difficulty. But little did she know that her greatest trial was yet to come.

*Now if we are children, then we are heirs—heirs of God
and co-heirs with Christ, if indeed we share in his sufferings
in order that we may also share in his glory.*

Romans 8:17

Wherever He Leads, I'll Go

"Take up thy cross and follow me,"
I heard my Master say;
"I gave my life to ransom thee,
Surrender your all today."

Wherever He leads I'll go,
Wherever He leads I'll go,
I'll follow my Christ who loves me so,
Wherever He leads I'll go.

Then Jesus said to his disciples, "Whoever wants
to be my disciple must deny themselves
and take up their cross and follow me."

Mark 8:34

---

5 A Journey to the Cross

Day 3

The tears continue to flow as I write this, but I believe in the end that God will restore Mom. I have to stand on that to get through each day. We know that we have difficult days ahead. There are no changes in Mom's condition. We have seen more doctors today than you could imagine—including a neurologist, a GBS specialist, a cardiologist, immunologist, pathologist, pulmonologist, respiratory therapist, physical therapist, occupational therapist, and a social worker. We are mentally and physically exhausted. Philippians 4:13 says "I can do all things through Christ who strengthens me." That is a promise we will continue to claim.

Day 5

Thankfully, we were able to develop a system to communicate with Mom. We now realize that she has the ability to raise her right eyebrow (indicating "yes") and move her lower jaw back and forth ever so slightly (to communicate "no"). So we are able to ask her yes and no questions to which she can respond. When she wants to spell a word, sentence or thought, we go through the alphabet letter by letter, and when we get to the correct letter in a word, she indicates "yes" by raising her eyebrow. We use a marker board and are hopeful that she will eventually be able to spell out complete sentences.

It sounds like a tedious process, yet we feel God has provided a miracle by giving Mom a way to communicate to us. It was as if her silence was finally broken. We were able to connect to her for the first time since this nightmare began. As much as we rejoice that we have a form of communication with her, it also gives us greater insight into the degree of suffering she is experiencing physically, emotionally and psychologically. That process of communication and that marker board has become the lifeline to connecting to Mom. We are so grateful.

These are some of the first words she spelled:

"DON'T LEAVE ME ALONE"
"ARM" (move my arm)
"BACK" (hurts)
"UP DOWN" (move her arms)
"FACE IS HOT"
"RAG COLD" (for her face)

"When you pass through the waters,
I will be with you;
and when you pass through the rivers,
they will not sweep over you.
When you walk through the fire,
you will not be burned;
the flames will not set you ablaze.
For I am the Lord, your God,
the Holy One of Israel, your Savior;
Do not be afraid, for I am with you."

Isaiah 43:2-3, 5

I once watched a fascinating documentary on the perils of attempting to climb Mt. Everest. The focus of the documentary was on the Sherpas who were from the area and highly trained and experienced in making the journey. They understood the terrain, the weather, the dangers, and most importantly—they had made the journey countless times. They knew how to prepare the climbers and how to protect them from danger. All Everest climbers know they must depend on the knowledge, expertise and guidance of the Sherpas—regardless of how much they themselves had read, studied or climbed before. Their lives depend on doing so.

I remember crying out to God and asking Him what was the purpose of everything we were going through. I heard Him reply very clearly: "You don't have to understand it, you just have to do it." I knew He was asking me to trust Him. I had to remind myself that I was being asked to trust the God of the universe— who fully knew the terrain of the mountain we were climbing, was fully-equipped to supply my every need on a treacherous journey, had traveled the journey of suffering before me, and was perfectly prepared to guide my every step. I was being asked to trust in the One who created me and knit me together in my mother's womb and who sacrificed His only beloved Son in order to have a personal relationship with me. He wanted me to place my trust in Him, who is sovereign and whose providence is always present and always at work. God knows exactly what I need at all times and in every circumstance. He was asking me to trust Him, and that's what I was desperately trying to do.

*We must choose to put our faith in
Christ—to believe in him—again and
again. After initially being "saved" then we
need to be "saved" every day, repeatedly—
from weariness, exhaustion, worry, despair,
hopelessness, etc. There is much to be
saved from, and his salvation is available
repeatedly if we seek it.*[4]

I once heard, "Your journey with God must take you to the cross."
A journey to the cross can include heartbreak, disappointment,
disease, disabilities, loss, tragedy, broken families and damaged
relationships. Mom's journey first took her to the cross when she
accepted Jesus as her Savior as a young child, but I also believe
that her journey had taken her to the cross many times throughout
the years, and she was once again at the cross of suffering. It was
incredibly difficult to watch her experience such agonizing pain,
as she lie trapped in a body that was holding her as a prisoner.
However, I was absolutely confident that the very faith that took
Mom to the cross of suffering had also taken her into the arms of
our loving, compassionate and faithful God.

---

*God is our refuge and strength, an ever-present help in trouble.
Therefore we will not fear, though the earth give way and the
mountains fall into the heart of the sea, though its waters roar and
foam and the mountains quake with their surging.*

Psalm 46:1-3

To God Be the Glory

To God be the glory, great things He hath done;
So loved He the world that He gave us His Son,
Who yielded His life an atonement for sin,
And opened the life gate that all may go in.

Praise the Lord, praise the Lord,
Let the earth hear His voice!
Praise the Lord, praise the Lord,
Let the people rejoice!
O come to the Father, through Jesus the Son,
And give Him the glory, great things He hath done.

To our God and Father be glory for ever and ever. Amen.

Philippians 4:20

---

6 For His Glory

Day 6

"Praise the Lord, praise the Lord! Let the earth hear His voice! Praise the Lord, praise the Lord! Let the people rejoice! O come to the Father through Jesus the Son and give Him the glory, great things He hath done!"

This is one of Mom's favorite hymns. We can just imagine her playing the piano and singing it aloud. So now we are claiming these words on her behalf. One of Mom's neurologists informed us today that her case falls in the 5% of all GBS cases in which the recovery is not expected to be as rapid or complete. We realize that this is only one doctor's prognosis, but as you can imagine, that was very difficult to hear.

Although we respect and appreciate scientific medicine and all it provides, we even more so fully trust and believe in the amazing healing power of God! Mom continues to communicate that she is in excruciating pain, so we also ask you to pray for her relief and comfort. As one sweet friend wrote to us, "We are storming the gates of heaven with prayers on her behalf." We realize that this is a long-term illness and that progress will be measured in weeks instead of days. We do know that Mom—even in her condition tonight—would echo the words of her beloved hymn, "Give Him the glory" for the great things He has done and will continue to do.

"...everyone who is called by my name,
whom I created for my glory, whom I formed and made."

Isaiah 43:7

Five years earlier I had faced my own battle—mine was with cancer. In a conversation with Mom during that time, I remember telling her that I had not questioned God's reasoning or asked Him "why" I had cancer. I will never forget her response: "That's because we know why—to bring glory to God." She was right. According to Scripture, we were created for God's glory, and that became my focus and my inspiration as I fought my own battle for life. I was confident that Mom still fully believed what she had said to me on that day years earlier. She didn't need to ask "why" she was facing such unimaginable pain and suffering in her life. She knew "why"—to bring glory to God. She had helped me claim that truth in my own life, and I chose to claim that truth for her life as well.

Now a man named Lazarus was sick. He was from Bethany, the
village of Mary and her sister Martha. (This Mary, whose brother
Lazarus now lay sick, was the same one who poured perfume on
the Lord and wiped his feet with her hair.) So the sisters sent word
to Jesus, "Lord, the one you love is sick." When he heard this, Jesus
said, "This sickness will not end in death. No, it is for God's glory so
that God's Son may be glorified through it." Now Jesus loved Martha
and her sister and Lazarus. So when he heard that Lazarus was
sick, he stayed where he was two more days, and then he said to his
disciples, "Let us go back to Judea."

John 11:1-4

When Jesus heard that his dear friend, Lazarus, was sick, he stayed away two days longer before going to him. He could have left right away—before Lazarus died—but he knew that Lazarus would have to face death and his family and friends would need to experience the unbearable grief of losing their loved one in order for God to receive the full glory when Jesus restored Lazarus' life. At the time it didn't make sense to those surrounding Jesus and those who loved Lazarus why Jesus had not come sooner to save him. But Jesus knew what was to come and God's purpose that was yet to unfold.

There are many times that I do not understand God's plan and am unable to fully comprehend how certain circumstances in my life will bring Him glory. As one pastor spoke of the trials we experience in life, he explained: "It is all for God's glory, yet we are only seeing the back side of His glory."[5] Even Moses was not allowed to fully see God's glory. God spoke to him out of a burning bush, from a pillar of cloud, and hid him behind a rock to protect him from the power of His full glory. God spoke to the Israelites from the fire in a cloud because they, too, were unable to witness His full glory without perishing. And Peter, James and John were covered by a bright cloud to protect them from witnessing the full glory of God descending upon Jesus. However, when we get to Heaven, God promises that we will see His face in His full glory, and then we will understand His plans and His ways.

They will see his face, and his name will be on their foreheads.
There will be no more night. They will not need the light of a lamp
or the light of the sun, for the Lord God will give them light.
And they will reign for ever and ever.

Revelation 22:3-4

I don't always understand the plan that God has for my life or for those I love, but I believe that everything that happens is ultimately to further reveal God's glory. Throughout our ordeal, my family discussed how God wanted us to use our experience to share His love and glory with others. I wondered how I would be able to give God glory when my heart was so broken and when my mind was filled with uncertainty about Mom's recovery. Then I realized I had the opportunity to honor Him every day in my relationships with my family members and with those caring for Mom. I was also giving God glory when I believed His promises of love and protection and when I trusted Him with my own life and with my mom's. I had to trust in God's plan and His promise that His full glory and purposes would one day be revealed to me when I get to Heaven and see His face.

Therefore we do not lose heart. Though outwardly we are wasting away, yet inwardly we are being renewed day by day. For our light and momentary troubles are achieving for us an eternal glory that far outweighs them all.
2 Corinthians 4:16-17

Turn Your Eyes upon Jesus

O soul, are you weary and troubled?
No light in the darkness you see?
There's a light for a look at the Savior,
And life more abundant and free!

Turn your eyes upon Jesus,
Look full in His wonderful face,
And the things of earth will grow strangely dim,
In the light of His glory and grace.

And let us run with endurance the race God has set before us.
We do this by keeping our eyes on Jesus, the champion
who initiates and perfects our faith.

Hebrews 12:1-2

7 Information Blackout

Day 8

We are asking for you to please pray for relief from the unbearable pain Mom has been experiencing throughout the night and this morning. We need the doctors to find an effective combination of medications, even though they have told us that it will have to be constantly adjusted. Some of the words Mom spelled for us today:

"PAIN"
"ALL ALONE" at night
"MOVE TO ANOTHER" [hospital] so we can stay with her at night
"I NEED TO DIE NOW"

Day 9

We felt everyone's prayers yesterday, and our prayers were answered as the increase in medicine brought Mom some relief from the pain. The doctors have put her on a constant drip of various medications that seem to be allowing her to rest a bit. The doctors are doing everything possible to help her. We meet with the GBS specialist tomorrow, and we have tough questions and difficult decisions ahead. Keep praying for that miracle.

Day 10

The GBS specialist said we are now looking at a 9-12 month recovery—instead of a 3-4 month recovery.

I knew Mom was desperate for an explanation of what was happening and what her prognosis would be. As her family, we shared in that desperation. We felt we were lost in what we often referred to as an "information blackout." All we knew was that Mom was suffering from an incredibly rare disease, and that her case was even more exceptional. We constantly searched the internet, made phone calls and read literature that could provide any insight or explanation.

No one really knows why Guillain-Barré strikes certain individuals. There is no vaccination for it, and there is no cure. It was just so hard to believe that with the abundance of information and research available to us through the internet and all the advancement in modern medicine, we found ourselves so desperate for information.

I remembered several years earlier when I had received the phone call that I had cancer. I sat in utter disbelief before turning on the computer to search for a more extensive explanation of my diagnosis, and I was overwhelmed by the immense amount of information available. It was such a stark contrast to the void of information on GBS.

He reveals deep and hidden things;
he knows what lies in darkness, and light dwells with him.

Daniel 2:22

God is all-knowing all the time. He was not part of the information blackout in Mom's situation, and He is all-knowing in every other circumstance I have faced and will face in my life. God reassured me of His sovereignty and that He was still orchestrating the events in my life. A friend gave me a devotional book a week after Mom became sick, and I decided to go back and read the entry for the day Mom first began to experience numbness in her fingers. The scripture was from Psalm 119:71: "It was good for me to be afflicted." Once again, I was reminded that God fully knew what was to come.

We go through difficult times in our lives when we don't understand. Even if we believe that everything that happens is ultimately for God's glory, it still doesn't always make sense. We still question God. We plead for Him to explain why something is happening and to give us some degree of understanding. Yet the answers often elude us. When I find myself in that place of crying out for understanding, I have to trust that God is constantly working and orchestrating the details of my life—even in the darkness of my circumstances—and remember that when I don't understand, He always does.

And we know that in all things God works for the good of those who love him, who have been called according to his purpose.

Romans 8:28

One of the foundational verses for my life is Romans 8:28. Having lived a life filled with joy and delight, as well as many times filled with heartache and grief, I cling to the promise that God is using all of it for "good" and for His purpose in my life.

"And we know that in all things God works for good…"

The good, the bad, the wonderful, the painful—*all things God works for good*. Thankfully, God leaves no doubt that He is talking about everything—every joyous moment, every heartbreaking experience, every broken relationship, every blessing, every painful loss, every celebration, every disappointment, every failure, every sin, every disaster—God is using every last bit of it for something good.

> *The extent is emphasized in the word "plantain" in the Greek, meaning all things. It is a comprehensive promise, and the context has no limits. There's nothing that qualifies the "all things," as null in void. It means absolutely what it says, all things work together for good. God takes anything and everything that occurs in a believer's life and makes it work together for the believer's ultimate good. This is the greatest promise that we can have in this life. There are absolutely no limits on this statement in this context. It is limitless.[6]*

"…of those who love him…"

God promises to orchestrate all things together for good and just asks that we love Him. That's it. This describes one of the most powerful promises in Scripture for those who are called into a relationship with God through Jesus Christ. God simply asks that we proclaim our love for Him, and then He promises to take care of the rest. One pastor elaborated further on the relationship between our love for God and His promise to work all things for good:

So Paul is not saying all things work for
good for Christians some of the time (when
their love for God is strong), and all things
don't work for good for Christians some of
the time (when their love for God is weak).
He is saying that for Christians—
the called, those whose hearts have been
brought from enmity to love for God—
all things work for good all the time.[7]

"…who have been called according to his purpose."

If I am trying to accomplish my own goals and purposes for my life without considering those God has set for me, then the peace and hope that He offers can elude me. I have found that my heart and mind are not always open to His reasoning and will for my life. It is easy to lose focus of His purpose when I so desperately want to pursue a different path or see a different outcome. Yet God's promise is clear that He is orchestrating everything in my life to accomplish His will, not always mine. I must constantly strive to trust in God's promise that all the circumstances in my life are accomplishing His will and purpose, which I do believe are always greater than my own.

Rather, as servants of God we commend ourselves in every way:
in great endurance; in troubles, hardships and distresses.

2 Corinthians 6:4

Mom wrote one final lesson for her Bible study two days before she was taken to the hospital. Mom had no way of knowing that God would use her last written lesson to speak a very personal message to those of us crying out for understanding and comfort. The subject was Lot's wife and how we needed to learn to accept the situation in which we find ourselves and not "look back." Because of the circumstances surrounding us when we first read it, its meaning was very profound and incredibly personal:

> *Can you see yourself ever looking back,*
> *regretting decisions, mourning lost*
> *opportunities, or yearning for ended*
> *relationships? When we look behind us,*
> *we can't see what is before us. We must*
> *leave the past behind, enjoy the present*
> *and plan for the future. God's mercy is*
> *always available to us, even in the worst*
> *of times, the most difficult situation,*
> *and the hardest of circumstances.*
> *He is there, stretching out His hand*
> *to lead us to safety.*[8]

In the midst of our own personal heartache, God reminded our family of His sovereignty. He knew Mom needed to be reminded of the truths she had written in that Bible study just days before she fell ill, and He knew we would need to find that lesson days later and be reminded of the very same truths. If we had read those words the day she had written them, their greater meaning and impact would have been lost on us. God used Mom's lesson on Lot's wife to provide us with her own words of comfort and hope— even when she was no longer able to speak them.

God knew what caused Mom to be stricken with GBS—even though no one else did—and God knew everything that we would be facing in our battle with such a devastating disease. Our family cried out for a very different outcome throughout Mom's illness, but God repeatedly revealed to us that He was accomplishing His will through everything that was happening. All things. Working together. For His purpose.

The Lord works out everything for his own ends—
even the wicked for a day of disaster.
In his heart a man plans his course,
but the Lord determines his steps.

Proverbs 16:4,9

Tis So Sweet to Trust in Jesus

Jesus, Jesus, how I trust Him!
How I've proved Him o'er and o'er
Jesus, Jesus, precious Jesus!
O for grace to trust Him more!

I'm so glad I learned to trust Thee,
Precious Jesus, Savior, Friend;
And I know that Thou art with me,
Wilt be with me to the end.

You will keep in perfect peace those whose
minds are steadfast, because they trust in you.

Isaiah 26:3

8 Colors of a Tapestry

Day 11 - 3:16 pm

Urgent: Pray now for Brenda and our family. Pray please...now.

Day 11 - 7:30 pm

Today has been an extremely difficult day. Mom's heart stopped, and the doctors revived her. She remains in very critical condition. Our family has three specific prayer requests at this time: Please pray for God's unfathomable peace for us all. Please pray for God's wisdom as we face very difficult decisions. We know that this would be Mom's prayer as well—that God will be glorified and that His will be done. We trust God completely.

The Hobbs Family

Mom's heart stopped beating. Was this it? Was she dying? It had been my first day back to work since she became sick. When I received the call that she went into cardiac arrest, I was devastated. I was two hours away and desperate to get to the hospital. I became frustrated that I had left the hospital. *What if I don't get a chance to say goodbye? What do I want her to know?* I was still unclear on exactly what had happened, and my heart and mind were filled with fear, doubt and uncertainty.

*For we are God's masterpiece. He has created us anew
in Christ Jesus, so we can do the good things
he planned for us long ago.*

Ephesians 2:10 NLT

I still remember the eloquent eulogy my mom spoke at my grandmother's funeral. She compared her life to a tapestry, woven together by the many different aspects of her personality and life experiences. Over the years I have thought more about the concept of a tapestry, as I have reflected on the experiences in my own life.

Colors are interesting. They can evoke emotion and represent different things to different people. Colors can demonstrate loyalty to a particular sports team or represent the seasons. Certain colors are seen as bright and uplifting while others can be viewed as dark or depressing. Some colors may be soothing, and some offensive. There are colors that I love to wear, but there are several colors that you will not find in my house or in my closet.

Just as there are colors I prefer and those I do not care for, so are the experiences in my life—which can also evoke emotion. There are events that have occurred in my life that have brought me great joy—marrying my husband, the birth of our children, the opportunity to work in ministry, and many other occasions. But there are also many circumstances that have caused me and my family great pain and sadness—including addiction, broken relationships, acts of violence, and the deaths of those we love. As I look at a tapestry, I am reminded that threads of every color are used to make such a beautiful works of art. The colors I prefer and those which I disdain are all part of the masterpiece.

I once looked at the back side of a tapestry, and it had hundreds of random threads hanging off and appeared incredibly haphazard. It was very unappealing and in no way represented the masterpiece revealed on the reverse side. Sometimes I feel that I am looking at the back side of the tapestry of my own life—not yet fully realizing the beauty that is being woven together. In my life God is the artist, and I must trust that He is weaving together all the circumstances in my life to create a masterpiece, including all my relationships, experiences, opportunities, trials and celebrations.

Many are the plans in a man's heart,
but it is the Lord's purpose that prevails.
Proverbs 19:21

The God of the universe created and loves me and is on His throne. He is looking down upon me and knows every detail about me and my life. He knows my deepest thoughts and my greatest fears. He knows my abilities and my weaknesses. He has equipped me and surrounded me with whom I need and what I need to make it through this journey of life. God is the artist of my life, and He is crafting me out of His creative and extraordinary love.

I am confident that no one loves me more than God, and I knew at the time that no one could possibly love my mom more than God. Even though the colors of the thread unfolding in my life were wrought with pain, I had to trust that our Creator was weaving a tapestry to make a masterpiece, and that one day we would be able to fully see and appreciate its beauty.

I lift up my eyes to the hills—
where does my help come from?
My help comes from the Lord,
the Maker of heaven and earth.
He will not let your foot slip—
he who watches over you will not slumber;
indeed, he who watches over Israel
will neither slumber nor sleep.
The Lord watches over you;
the Lord is your shade at your right hand;
the sun will not harm you by day,
nor the moon by night.
The Lord will keep you from all harm—
he will watch over your life;
the Lord will watch over your coming and going
both now and forevermore.

Psalm 121

I Need Thee Every Hour

I need Thee ev'ry hour,
Most gracious Lord;
No tender voice like Thine
Can peace afford.

I need Thee, O I need Thee!
Ev'ry hour I need Thee;
O bless me now, my Saviour!
I come to Thee.

Let us then approach the throne of grace with confidence,
so that we may receive mercy and find grace to help us
in our time of need.

Hebrews 4:16

---

9 My Heart Hurts

Day 12

Mom survived a very difficult day yesterday and also the night. Today we truly believe it is a miracle that she is with us and that she is able to once again flicker an eyebrow to communicate to us—even if it is ever so slightly. At this time, the doctors have reiterated that Mom's case of GBS is "catastrophic" and is one of the "absolutely most severe" of all documented cases. However, we are still hopeful and prayerful that the remaining plasma exchanges and the upcoming IVIg injections will be helpful to her condition and prognosis.

We are asking our "Earth Angels" to continue praying for her to experience God's inexplicable peace, relief from the pain, and the strength and patience to endure her journey to recovery. God's love and grace have been poured out upon our family and Mom through your prayers, words of encouragement, and your unbelievable love for Mom. All these things have sustained us through these past days, and we know they will continue to do so. We are continuing to put Mom in God's hands, knowing that His love for her far surpasses all of our love combined. We truly do trust Him with her life.

He heals the brokenhearted and binds up their wounds.

Psalm 147:3

It was a terribly dark day. When Mom's heart stopped and she had to be resuscitated, we were gripped with fear and uncertainty. We had tried so hard to remain positive and hopeful, and we suddenly found ourselves feeling helpless and hopeless. My heart truly hurt.

> *Broken heart syndrome is a temporary*
> *heart condition that's often brought on*
> *by stressful situations, such as the death*
> *of a loved one. People with broken heart*
> *syndrome may have sudden chest pain or*
> *think they're having a heart attack.*
> *In broken heart syndrome, there's a*
> *temporary disruption of your heart's*
> *normal pumping function, while the*
> *remainder of the heart functions normally*
> *or with even more forceful contractions.*[9]

The physical condition of heartache is real and can be agonizing. It is a deep, aching pain that cannot always be alleviated by friends, music, laughter, distraction, or even prayer. It is a condition in which intense sadness relentlessly grips your heart and does not let go. Heartache can occur when we experience the loss of a relationship or a loved one, when we feel betrayed, rejected or abandoned, or when devastation or disappointment descend upon our lives. And when we experience such deep pain and sorrow, we may wonder if we will ever find our way out of the darkness that has overcome us.

In the Bible, Jacob was consumed with grief when he thought Joseph had been killed. Job experienced intense heartache when he suffered the immense loss of his health, his children, his wealth, and his friends. David suffered heartbreak when he recognized the depths of his sin. Even Jesus was heartbroken when he saw the suffering of Mary and Martha following the death of Lazarus. And anticipating his own crucifixion, Jesus experienced such anguish that he sweat drops of blood. God, too, knows our heartache. Not only did He experience suffering through Jesus, but one can only imagine the grief He experienced as He watched His son being crucified. As our Heavenly Father and a God of mercy and compassion (2 Corinthians 1:3), His heart is surely filled with sadness, as He witnesses the pain and suffering of His children.

The righteous cry out, and the Lord hears them;
he delivers them from all their troubles.

Psalm 34:17

One of my dearest friends suddenly and tragically lost her young daughter to a devastating illness. The heartache I experienced watching my friend be overwhelmed by such grief and loss was truly agonizing. I am still unable to fully understand the intensity of the heartache she has continued to experience, but I find comfort in knowing that God fully comprehends the depth of her pain, and He continues to pour His compassion and mercy upon her life and her family. Because His love for each of us is boundless and immeasurable, I believe that when our hearts ache, God's heart aches as well, and it is out of His abundant love and compassion that He pours down His grace and strength to help us through our grief and despair.

So when we endure these heartbreaks
ourselves—rejection, betrayal,
abandonment—we don't walk through
them alone. God has walked that road
himself. And in some mysterious way, when
our hearts are broken, we're given new
insight into the very character of God.[10]

Jacob mourned the loss of his son and remained faithful to the calling of God in his life. Job experienced deep heartache, but instead of rejecting God, he worshiped Him. As David recognized the depths of his sin, he repented and grieved, and his faith was strengthened. Following Jesus' tears of despair, he performed one of his greatest miracles in Scripture and raised Lazarus from the dead. Even though he experienced intense anguish anticipating his own crucifixion, he was obedient to follow God's will for his life.

Your most profound and intimate
experiences of worship will likely be in your
darkest days—when your heart is broken,
when you feel abandoned, when you're out
of options, when the pain is great—
and you turn to God alone.[11]

During the days and weeks that I helplessly watched my mom suffer, my heart physically ached. I know that there will be roads which will lead to even more heartache in my journey through life, and I will surely continue to cry out to God for understanding and relief from the pain. Yet through it all, I pray that I will be faithful to worship Him even in times of trouble. When we experience heartache we can be certain that God sees our despair, hears our prayers, and is filled with compassion. Therefore, I will choose to place my trust in Him, in His faithfulness, and in His enduring love.

Praise be to the God and Father of our Lord Jesus Christ,
the Father of compassion and the God of all comfort,
who comforts us in all our troubles, so that we can comfort those
in any trouble with the comfort we ourselves receive from God.

2 Corinthians 1:3-4

Trust and Obey

When we walk with the Lord in the light of His Word,
What a glory He sheds on our way!
While we do His good will, He abides with us still,
And with all who will trust and obey.

Trust and obey, for there's no other way
To be happy in Jesus, but to trust and obey.

Lord Almighty, blessed is the one who trusts in You.

Psalm 84:12

---

10 Writing in the Dirt

Day 14

Tonight Mom needs rest. The doctors are still unable to consistently control her pain, and she continues to communicate that it is unbearable. They took her off all pain meds to conduct another nerve conduction test to which she still had no response. She has had elevated blood pressure, which could be associated with the intense pain. We absolutely believe in, hope for, and pray for God's miraculous deliverance for Mom from this pain and suffering. We fully trust in our God and Savior to answer our prayers and pour down grace and mercy upon Mom.

"NINE ONE ONE" (call for help)
"FLY HOSPITAL" (fly her to another hospital where they can control the pain)

Day 15

"GO WITH GOD"

Day 17

Mom was communicative throughout the day. She was in less pain but still very discouraged and not wanting to fight. According to the doctor, her nerves have been severely damaged, and she will spend months on life support. Our family needs to prepare for and understand, as the doctor stated, that she could be "profoundly impaired forever." There is a high probability she will be neurologically impaired for the rest of her life. We

discussed our dilemma with the doctor because we are absolutely
certain that her wishes are to not live this way.

"KILL ME, JOE" Her respiratory therapist, Joe, has the
ability to turn off her ventilator.
"DIE"
"DEAF" She was having trouble hearing.
"TRUDGE" tired
"TOPHET" some place, condition, etc., likened to hell[12]
"FERAL" causing death; fatal[13]

Find rest, O my soul, in God alone. My hope comes from Him.
He alone is my rock and my salvation. He is my fortress.
I will not be shaken.

Psalm 62:5-6

Mom continued to express her desires to be taken off life support.
Although she was ready to "go with God" and to "die," we were
not yet convinced that her condition was irreversible. For years
Mom had been adamant that she would never want to live
dependent upon life support, but we still needed to bring in more
doctors and consult more specialists before facing that decision.
Several members of our family were making arrangements to fly
to Philadelphia to attend a conference where the world's leading
doctors and researchers on GBS were gathered, as we searched
for a different answer and a more hopeful prognosis. We were not
prepared to concede.

Lord, hear my prayer, listen to my cry for mercy;
in your faithfulness and righteousness
come to my relief.

Psalm 143:8-11

Sometimes we are waiting for God to write in the sky, and perhaps He has already written in the dirt. When the answer is not one we desire, we may keep searching and hoping it will change. Or perhaps we don't see His response because we are not yet prepared to accept it. We may be missing God's answers because He provides them in creative and unexpected ways.

Throughout the Bible, God demonstrates His ability to provide for His people's needs in unique and extraordinary ways. He designed a rainbow as a reminder of His covenant to never destroy the earth again by a flood. Throughout their journey in the desert, the Israelites were guided by God in the form of a cloud as they set out from Egypt, and a cloud of fire provided light during the night by which to travel. The fortified walls of Jericho crumbled at the sound of a trumpet. God saved Daniel from ravenous lions and spared three faithful men from being consumed by fire in a furnace. Jonah survived three days in the belly of a fish. God even provided food for thousands of people with two fish and a few loaves of bread.

Our journey was also filled with large—and small—reminders that God's provision for our family was both abundant and creative. When I began to feel discouraged or disheartened, God would repeatedly remind me of the ways He had already been working and providing what we needed, when we needed it.

When Mom returned to the emergency room the morning she became paralyzed, the same doctor was treating her that had helped her several nights earlier. That expedited the process of ordering the appropriate tests and procedures necessary to reach a diagnosis.

When we made the decision to transfer her to another hospital, the ease in which the logistics aligned was nothing short of a miracle. What could have been difficult and cumbersome was, instead, seamless and simple.

When the doctors resuscitated Mom the day her heart stopped, we were once again reminded of His grace and mercy—another example of how He made His works and wonders apparent even through the most difficult times.

I remember one day at the hospital when my sister and I were discussing how we needed to get some hair bows for Mom. That same evening I was at my son's little league baseball game, and a young girl came up to the stands with a basket of homemade bows for sale—at a baseball game! We bought five bows that night and had to smile at God's provision.

We learned that the international conference on GBS was only held every two years and was scheduled to begin one month after Mom was diagnosed. The conference was sold out, but several people from my family were able to attend.

Mom spent her life playing and singing hymns. She had committed their words to memory and found great solace in them. Now her days were filled with those same sacred melodies and lyrics, once again providing her comfort in what was certainly the most difficult time of her life.

Mom also always loved words. The Scrabble Queen—that's what we called her. Often if there was a lull in our family vacations or even at home, Mom would convince one of the kids or grandkids to take a shot at beating her in Scrabble (which was practically impossible). She was notorious for using words we did not know. Her response would be: "It's a Scrabble word." She eventually became more proficient on the computer, and her attention turned toward the electronic version of the game. It would be safe to say that one of her greatest passions in life was Scrabble. Now as she lay in a hospital bed unable to speak, her proficiency and patience for spelling with individual letters became one of the greatest examples of God's provision and grace during that time. One afternoon in the hospital, we thought Mom was confused when she repeatedly spelled the word "feral" because it most commonly refers to a wild animal. Then a friend of ours looked it up online using his phone and realized that another form of the word means "causing death; fatal." Of course she knew exactly what she was saying. It just took us a while to understand. From then on when she spelled a word unknown to us, instead of doubting her, we would simply ask: "Is it a Scrabble word?"

And this same God who takes care of me
will supply all your needs from his glorious riches,
which have been given to us in Christ Jesus.
Philippians 4:19 NLT

When I take time to reflect on the creative ways God has responded to my prayers, I am reminded of His provision which has often come in unexpected ways and not always from the direction I was expecting. I was so eagerly looking to Heaven awaiting God's miraculous healing of Mom's body, that I had to be careful not to miss the daily miracles (the writing in the dirt) that He was performing right before my eyes.

I want to remember how God has demonstrated His faithfulness in my life in the past and how is He doing so today, so that I will have the confidence to face the adversities in life that will once again come knocking at my door. When I am struggling to see the answers which I am so desperately seeking, God reminds me that He hears me and answers me. Each time my strength melts into weariness and my clarity dissolves into confusion, God assures me that He is supplying everything I need and often in ways I am not expecting—like bows at a baseball game.

"The mountains be shaken and the hills be removed,
yet my unfailing love for you will not be shaken
nor my covenant of peace be removed," says the LORD,
who has compassion on you.

Isaiah 54:10

Have Thine Own Way

Have Thine own way, Lord! Have Thine own way!
Thou art the Potter, I am the clay.
Mold me and make me after Thy will,
While I am waiting, yielded and still.

Have Thine own way, Lord! Have Thine own way!
Wounded and weary, help me, I pray!
Power, all power, surely is Thine!
Touch me and heal me, Savior divine.

But now, O Lord, thou art our father;
we are the clay, and thou our potter;
and we all are the work of thy hand.

Isaiah 64:8 KJV

11 Your Will Be Done

Day 19

    "SING"
    "LOUDER"
    "SING TO GOD"
    "SCARED"
    "TALKING TO ANGELS"

Day 20

    "I WANT TO SMILE"

Day 22

    "MY LIFE IS OVER"
    "PLEASE HELP ME BREATHE"
    "LIFE IS GONE"
    "THANK YOU" to a nurse who washed her face

Day 24 - 4:28 pm

Mom was just taken back for surgery. They are performing a tracheotomy on her in order to move the ventilation from her mouth to a trach tube in her neck. They are also placing her feeding tube directly into her stomach. Both of these procedures should lead to Mom being more comfortable. The surgery is expected to last several hours. We ask that you please pray for strength for her body and for wisdom and guidance for the surgeons. Thank you for your prayers.

Day 24 - 5:45 pm

Thank you, God! The surgeon just came out and reported that Mom's surgery went very well. They successfully moved the feeding tube and placed the trach. She will be in ICU for the next two days. Once the ICU doctors release her, we will consider moving her to a long-term critical care facility where they can continue to closely monitor her condition.

---

*Do not conform to the pattern of this world,
but be transformed by the renewing of your mind.
Then you will be able to test and approve what God's will is—
his good, pleasing and perfect will.*

Romans 12:2

I have learned that my life is not about me. Instead, it is about God and His plan for me. When I was seven years old, I asked Jesus to be the Lord of my life. Since that young age, my faith and trust in Jesus has grown and matured, yet the fact that I gave him authority over my life has remained unchanged. As I grew from that young child, I have learned that God doesn't promise to remove us *from* our circumstances, but He promises to carry us *through* our circumstances. He assures us that He will equip us with everything we need to navigate this often difficult and troubled life. As a child of God, I have access to His hope, wisdom, peace, patience, endurance and strength, and by surrendering my life to Him, I have gained the wealth and provision of the God of the universe.

"This, then, is how you should pray: 'Our Father in heaven, hallowed be your name, your kingdom come, your will be done, on earth as it is in heaven. Give us today our daily bread. And forgive us our debts, as we also have forgiven our debtors. And lead us not into temptation, but deliver us from the evil one."

Matthew 6:9-13

In the Lord's Prayer, we are taught to praise God and ask for Him to provide for our needs. We seek His forgiveness and His help to forgive those who have sinned against us, and we ask God to protect our hearts from evil. But Jesus also teaches us to pray that God's "will be done, on earth as it is in heaven." We often pray this prayer, but do we truly desire for God's will to prevail in our lives?

We don't need to tell God what we need.
We need to ask God for what we need.[14]

I am learning to pray that God would conform my will to His will, instead of praying that He would conform His will to mine. There are many times that I believe I know what is best for myself or for others, yet I only have a limited, human and worldly perspective. God has the perspective of the all-knowing Creator. He can see from eternity backwards to eternity forward. He knows the number of hairs on my head and every single thing that has and will happen in my life. He knew when I was to be born, and He knows when I will breathe my last breath. He has a heavenly perspective. Yet sometimes I struggle to trust Him and His perfect wisdom. I will continue to pray for the desires of my heart, but I will also pray that God would conform my heart and mind to His, and that He would further prepare me for His will in my life.

When my plan for my life aligns with God's, and my desires are fulfilled for myself and for those I love, I don't struggle with His will. But what if God's plan includes adversity or suffering? It can be difficult to comprehend that His plan would also include trials and heartache. Although pain and suffering were first introduced into this world by Satan, God, in His sovereignty, uses what Satan intends for harm and destruction to accomplish His purposes.

Yet it was the Lord's will to crush him [Jesus] and cause him to suffer, and though the Lord makes his life an offering for sin...

Isaiah 53:10

Jesus' own suffering and death illustrate for us how God claims what Satan intends for evil and instead uses it to fulfill prophecy and achieve His divine purposes. It is difficult to understand why there is suffering in the world, and we may questions God's love for us when we face trials and adversity in our lives. Yet there is a confidence in knowing that it was also God's will for Jesus—His own Son whom He deeply loved—to experience unimaginable suffering. Jesus prayed with great anguish before being arrested and crucified that he not have to face the pain and suffering of the cross, but ultimately he humbly submitted to God's plan for his life.

"Father, if you are willing, take this cup from me; yet not my will, but yours be done." An angel from heaven appeared to him and strengthened him. And being in anguish, he prayed more earnestly, and his sweat was like drops of blood falling to the ground.

Luke 22:42-44

Thankfully for us, Jesus was willing to surrender to God's will and be crucified for our sins and be raised from the dead, so that we might have eternal life. There are times I, too, pray for God to deliver me from my suffering, and I pray the same for those whom I love. Sometimes it is God's will to do so, but there are also times, in His immense love for me, that He is calling me to be obedient and to accept His will and whatever that may encompass.

> *The will of God will not take us*
> *where the grace of God will not sustain us.*[15]

At the time of his crucifixion, Jesus' family, friends, and even his disciples were unable to comprehend why he had to suffer such a horrific death although he had done nothing wrong, but God had a plan and a purpose that those who loved Jesus could not yet see. Through their own painful grief, they had to find a way to place their trust in God and believe in His love for His Son. They had to trust that there was a perfect plan and purpose in God's divine will.

> *The Lord longs to be gracious to you;*
> *he rises to show you compassion.*
> Isaiah 30:18

Just as in Jesus' life, the trials and heartache we face in our own lives are not apart from God's love, grace, comfort and compassion. Our Heavenly Father provides everything we need to walk through the difficulties we must endure. Not only does He walk alongside us on the road of suffering, but when we feel we cannot continue on, He picks us up in His loving arms and carries us.

Lord, send me anywhere, only go with me.
Lay any burden on me, only sustain me.
Sever any ties save the tie that binds me to
Thy heart. My Jesus, my King, my life, my
all, I again dedicate my whole self to Thee.[16]

Surrendering to God's will in my life is not always easy. I have to remind myself that God's love for me and for those I love far exceeds my own. His perspective on our lives is one which I cannot envision, and His ability to know what is best for each of us surpasses my own understanding. When God's will includes times of heartache and sorrow, I can trust Him to provide comfort and peace that is beyond what I am able to comprehend. Therefore, as I strive to trust God's will for my own life, I will also endeavor to trust Him with the lives of those whom I so deeply love.

For it has been granted to you on behalf of Christ
not only to believe in him, but also to suffer for him.

Philippians 1:29

Life is hard. Our world tries to tell us that if we are doing the right thing, then life shouldn't be difficult, but that is inconsistent with what the Bible teaches. As a matter of fact, Scripture tells us that if we are faithful to God's calling, that we, like Jesus, will face hardships, suffering and even persecution. And, like Jesus, we will overcome. My trials are the ideal opportunities for God's strength to be made perfect in my weakness and to highlight His grace, goodness and glory. Hardships are not only for those who have sinned and made poor choices but also for the faithful who are diligently seeking God's will for their lives. As we prepare to enter the kingdom of God, He reminds us that we will encounter many trials on the road to that place of glory.

We must go through many hardships
to enter the kingdom of God.

John 16:33

What a Friend We Have in Jesus

What a friend we have in Jesus,
All our sins and griefs to bear!
What a privilege to carry
Everything to God in prayer!
Oh, what peace we often forfeit,
Oh, what needless pain we bear,
All because we do not carry
Everything to God in prayer!

Have we trials and temptations?
Is there trouble anywhere?
We should never be discouraged—
Take it to the Lord in prayer.
Can we find a friend so faithful,
Who will all our sorrows share?
Jesus knows our every weakness;
Take it to the Lord in prayer.

"I no longer call you servants, because a servant does not know
his master's business. Instead, I have called you friends."

John 15:15

---

12 My Questions. God's Answers.

Day 25

"Rejoice always. Pray continually, give thanks in all circumstances; for this is God's will for you in Christ Jesus.... Reject whatever is harmful." (I Thessalonians 5:16-22).

These scriptures ring so true in our hearts. Please continue to pray. Pray unceasingly for renewed strength, full recovery and perfect peace. Mother will be transferred tomorrow to a critical care facility closer to home. Please pray for the transfer process and especially for pain relief during the transfer and relocation. We all look forward to a change in scenery. Pray also for the team of caregivers that we will encounter there. We know that God goes before us preparing the way. He remains faithful.

Day 26

> "WHERE AM I"
> "NAME OF HOSPITAL"

The transport was incredibly painful for Mom, and it was very difficult for Dad to watch Mom suffer so greatly. When they arrived, she was very tired. She wanted to know where she was and complained of severe pain. By the afternoon, she began bleeding through her mouth and nose, and her neck began to swell. There was a concern that the rough ambulance ride caused a tear in her esophagus and that surgery may have to be performed. She was taken again by ambulance to the hospital nearby and admitted to ICU. We have decided that if surgery is required, we will refuse. It would be too much to put Mom through that. We are preparing to say goodbye to her.

Day 27

The doctors were able to stabilize Mom, but she remains in ICU. Our family gathered to meet with the attending physician. We sat around a table in the conference room and expressed our desire to honor Mom's wishes not to continue living in this state. When we explained to him how alert, coherent and aware she had been, he was very doubtful of her ability to comprehend her circumstances. He said it would be highly unusual for someone in the severity of her condition to be of sound mind, especially after being in ICU, on a ventilator, and so heavily medicated for nearly a month. We welcomed his professional opinion after his assessment of her. He agreed to do so the following morning. He said that if Mom was not of sound mind, he would rely upon us to express what her wishes would be for her life if she were not able to clearly communicate them.

My son, if you accept my words and store up my commands within you, turning your ear to wisdom and applying your heart to understanding—indeed, if you call out for insight and cry aloud for understanding, and if you look for it as for silver and search for it as for hidden treasure, then you will understand the fear of the LORD and find the knowledge of God. For the LORD gives wisdom; from his mouth come knowledge and understanding.

Proverbs 2:1-6

Once again we believed that we were going to lose Mom, and I desperately needed God to remind me of His faithfulness and His unwavering love for me and for her. There were so many times that I cried out for understanding. I struggled to comprehend God's ways and reasoning, and I desperately sought to gain His perspective on the tragedy that continued to unfold in our lives.

I have often wondered what God thinks when I repeatedly question His faithfulness, when I doubt His purpose or plan, or when I respond to life's hardships with frustration and despair. I have since learned that some of God's most faithful servants questioned and doubted during times of suffering, as they struggled to comprehend their circumstances. God knows that we are human and that we are experiencing life from a very limited perspective, and the Bible tells us that God expects us to "cry aloud for understanding."

[John] sent his disciples to ask [Jesus], "Are you the one who is to come, or should we expect someone else?"

Matthew 11:2

An example of God's faithful yet doubting servant is seen in the life of John the Baptist. John prophesied the coming of Jesus. He baptized Jesus in the desert and witnessed God affirming that Jesus was, indeed, His son. Yet later when John was arrested and sat in a dark, lonely prison cell, he began to question if Jesus was truly the Messiah after all. But that didn't make sense. John had been called by God as a prophet to prepare the way for Jesus. When Jesus asked John to baptize him, "John tried to deter him, saying, "I need to be baptized by you." (Matthew 3:14). John knew Jesus and knew his purpose was to bring the world salvation. Yet the events in John's life were not unfolding as he had anticipated. He was enduring unexpected persecution and suffering. He was imprisoned and facing almost certain death. As his heart became filled with despair, confusion and hopelessness, he began to question the divinity of Jesus and God's purpose in everything that was happening. John's heart was filled with doubt and questions.

Jesus replied, "Go back and report to John what you hear and see: The blind receive sight, the lame walk, those who have leprosy are cleansed, the deaf hear, the dead are raised, and the good news is proclaimed to the poor."

Matthew 11:4-5

Jesus' response was not to scold John or condemn him for his wavering faith. Instead, he told John's disciples to return to him in prison and remind him of all of the works he was performing. Jesus' deeds would prove that he truly was the Messiah. In times of doubt we also need to remember what Jesus has done, and all that he is capable of doing. We must remind ourselves of his love for us, the depth of his compassion, and his willingness to die that we might have eternal life. We must remember his ability to heal, to save, and to give life. Remembering these qualities about Jesus offers us hope and confidence because we have a Savior who is Lord over all—all sickness, all pain, and all suffering.

Jesus said, "Truly I tell you, among those born of women there has not risen anyone greater than John the Baptist."

Matthew 11:11

Even after John's questioning and doubting, Jesus did not express disappointment in John but instead proclaimed to the crowd gathered that he was a man of great faith.

Best-selling author and pastor Rick Warren, and his wife, Kay, were interviewed following the death of their 27 year-old son, Matthew, who died by a self-inflicted gunshot wound. Kay admitted that even they questioned: "Did we ask, 'God, how could you allow this?' Absolutely. But our faith is strong." Rick also said: "Some things in life you are not going to get the answer to. What I get from God is not explanations, it's comfort."[17]

For just as we share abundantly in the sufferings of Christ,
so also our comfort abounds through Christ.

2 Corinthians 1:5

When I ask "why" or cry out for understanding, and when I doubt God and His plan for my life or the life of someone I love, God answers me with a response of love and compassion. He is not disappointed, frustrated or angry. God understands that there will be times that I will fall into the darkness of doubt. When I question, He answers by reminding me of His past faithfulness and provision, not only in my own life, but also in the lives of those around me. I am reminded of His character and His many acts of faithfulness that are recorded throughout the pages of Scripture.

God reminded me that it was okay to question what was happening and why. He knew that I trusted Him with my life and with Mom's, and that I believed everything that happens in life is for His glory. He knew that I had faith in His plan and His will, but

He also understood my moments of uncertainty and despair. He knew I needed to be reminded of all the deeds He had done in our lives over the past weeks, as well as His compassion, power and sovereignty displayed throughout the pages of Scripture. In response to my doubt and confusion, God reassured me of the depths of His love and faithfulness—the response of a gracious and loving Father.

Answer me, Lord, out of the goodness of your love;
in your great mercy turn to me.

Psalm 69:16

Rock of Ages

Rock of Ages, cleft for me,
Let me hide myself in Thee;
Let the water and the blood,
From Thy wounded side which flowed,
Be of sin the double cure,
Cleanse me from its guilt and power.

While I draw this fleeting breath,
When my eyelids close in death,
When I soar to worlds unknown,
See Thee on Thy judgment throne;
Rock of Ages, cleft for me,
Let me hide myself in Thee.

The Lord is my rock, my fortress and my deliverer.

Psalm 18:2

13 Stars at Night

Day 28

The speech therapist came to evaluate Mom's communication needs. Once she saw our system for communicating and how effective it was, she said that she was extremely impressed and did not have anything more to offer. When she began to leave, Mom indicated "NO. NO. NO." and wanted to communicate something to her.

Mom then spelled out: "I WANT TO SPEAK." The therapist explained to her that she would be unable to talk with the trach, to which Mom spelled out: "WE WERE TOLD I COULD TALK" (with the trach). Mom remembered that the doctor at the previous hospital had explained that a different valve could be placed on the trach so that she would be able to talk. The therapist then understood her question and explained that she was not yet in a condition to have the valve changed.

The attending physician came in later in the morning to evaluate her mental abilities. He said he was completely confident and quite surprised that she was, indeed, completely coherent and of sound mind.

From Dad:

Tonight Brenda is resting in the ICU. The physicians and nurses have done an excellent job of caring for her and managing her pain. They will continue to monitor her condition very closely, and she will remain in ICU at least for the next three days.

God has, indeed, shown us His compassion, as our family and Brenda have had a restful day and what we hope will be a restful night. We really appreciate the care and concern you have shown for our family and for Brenda. All of your scriptures, words of encouragement and prayers have been very uplifting.

Carey

Day 29

Mom spelled "FAITH."

In this you greatly rejoice, though now for a little while you may have had to suffer grief in all kinds of trials. These have come so that your faith—of greater worth than gold, which perishes even though refined by fire— may be proved genuine and may result in praise, glory and honor when Jesus Christ is revealed.

1 Peter 1:6-7

As I look back on that week in my life, I am reminded of how many times in my life God has sustained me through painful and unthinkable circumstances. Yet His grace and compassion have always been abundant and sufficient. Mom and Dad had said on many occasions that they knew very few families who experienced the amount and depth of trials that our family had faced, but Mom's battle with GBS was unlike anything we had ever faced before.

Give thanks to him who made the heavenly lights—
His faithful love endures forever. The sun to rule the day,
His faithful love endures forever. And the moon and stars
to rule the night. His faithful love endures forever.

Psalm 136:7-9 NLT

One evening in Colorado several years ago, I was mesmerized by the beauty of the stars which shined especially bright that night. I began to think about how those very stars would gradually disappear, as the sun would begin to rise the following morning. They would not move from their places in the heavens, nor would their brilliance dissipate, but I would no longer be able to see them. The stars, fixed in their places in the sky, are only visible on a dark night, and they are impossible to see with the naked eye in daylight.

The stars are a great illustration for the character of God and His love for us. God is steadfast, never changing, and He is there whether or not I can see Him. His faithfulness, love, strength, hope and peace, as well as everything else He provides me, are present in the light of celebration, as well as in the darkness of pain. The deeper the darkness, the more illuminated His character and provision shine in my life.

"I the Lord do not change."

Malachi 3:6

Even when we do not reach out to God or acknowledge His presence, He is still there. Even when I fail to claim His strength, His mercy or His help, they are always available to me. Although the times I request God's assistance in my life may fluctuate, His willingness to help me and His ability to do so never waver. As I face times of joy as well as despair, and as I stand strong in my faith and then find myself doubting, God is my Rock. He is my solid foundation. He is my hope. He is never-changing. He is the brilliant light that shines forth from the stars in both daylight and in darkness.

Stars in the Darkness
by Cindy Janecka

I need Your mercy. I cry out for Your grace.
What I need, Lord, is to see Your face.
I ask for Your spirit to wash over me.
You're what I need, Lord, to finally be free.

To my mind and my thoughts, I'm a captive in chains.
In the quiet of night, they are all that remain.
I try to escape and try to be free.
But I know it will take more than I have in me.

Just like a child, Lord, I stumble and I fall.
But I now stand before You and surrender my all.
I am falling into Your arms—take my heart and my mind,
I'm desperate for the freedom I can never seem to find.

I'm lost in the darkness—Your hope and love are my light
And just like the stars, they appear brightest in the night.[18]

How Firm a Foundation

How firm a foundation, ye saints of the Lord,
Is laid for your faith in His excellent Word!
What more can He say than to you He hath said,
You, who unto Jesus for refuge have fled?

Fear not, I am with thee, O be not dismayed,
For I am thy God and will still give thee aid;
I'll strengthen and help thee, and cause thee to stand
Upheld by My righteous, omnipotent hand.

God's solid foundation stands firm.

2 Timothy 2:19

14 Prepared for Battle

Day 31

Mom was moved back to the critical care hospital late this afternoon. She did well on the transfer and is now settled in. Her limited facial responses (her ability to move her jaw and eyebrow) have become significantly weaker. Later in the evening Mom spelled to Dad:

"BYE" He replied that he was not yet ready to leave her.
"MIND" He refused.

Day 33

Mom had a good night, but she began complaining of incredibly painful bladder spasms. She cried throughout the day and winced in pain. When she cries, her right eyelids quivers. She seems to be getting her days and nights confused. She sleeps most of the day but is often awake at night. She told Dad that her pain was an 11 on a scale 1-10. She mostly wanted Dad to hold her hand.

"I AM DYING" because of so much pain

Day 35

"ROOF"
"HELI"copter

Do you want a helicopter to come get you?

Yes.

Where do you want it to take you?

"HOSPITAL" back to ICU where they managed her pain more effectively

Mom has had another difficult week. The doctors have had a hard time effectively managing her pain despite their best efforts. She has been slightly more alert but has communicated significantly less than in weeks past. Every doctor who has cared for Mom (in 4 different hospitals) agrees that there are no documented cases of GBS to the severity of hers. We have gotten an additional opinion from a neurologist in New York and are waiting on responses from doctors in Ohio, Houston and Dallas. This weekend two of our family members are attending the international GBS conference in Pennsylvania in an effort to talk to more specialists who may have seen a similar case. We even have a friend who is contacting a physician overseas on our behalf. We are desperate for information that is relevant specifically to Mom's case. After nearly six weeks, we continue to see her worsen in ways which greatly concern us and her doctors. Please pray for the following: God would provide wisdom for the doctors, and that they would be able to effectively and consistently manage her pain; we would find doctors who have relevant and useful information about a case similar to Mom's; God would continue to pour out His unfailing mercy upon Mom, Dad and our family; and God would continue to receive glory through our heartache and trials. He has been faithful to provide all we have needed to endure this battle for these past weeks, and we are grateful.

Your word is a lamp for my feet, a light on my path.

Psalm 119:105

Throughout the days and week that Mom lay in a hospital bed and in unmanageable pain, I often found it difficult to find quiet time alone with God to pray and read my Bible. Reading the Bible had grown to become an important part of my daily routine, but my life was suddenly very chaotic. I slept very little in order to take care of my children and my own family's needs, so that I could be with Mom as much as possible. Yet through it all I felt intimately connected to God, and I wondered how I could experience God's presence so powerfully and consistently when I was spending so little time alone with Him or studying the Bible. Then I realized that everything I had learned about God and all the Scriptures I had studied over the years were written onto my heart and into my soul. Instead of reading about who God is and what He can do for me, I was *living* it. I was *experiencing* God in a way I never had before.

> *The time to prepare for a storm is before the storm hits, not in the midst of the storm.*[19]

I was reminded of the importance of storing up God's truths and forging a close relationship with Him, so when disappointment, heartbreak and devastation overcome my life, I am prepared and equipped. Even though the amount of time I was able to devote to daily Bible study and prayer was limited, the strength and the comfort of God's Word were never more powerfully felt and experienced.

For everything that was written in the past was written to teach us, so that through the endurance taught in the Scriptures and the encouragement they provide we might have hope.

Romans 15:4

Several years ago my husband, children and I had the opportunity to live with my parents for several months, and I learned that each morning Mom and Dad sat at the kitchen table reading their Bibles as they began their day. For the past several years, Mom had been reading a daily chronological Bible. When she was in the hospital, I was at their house one day and noticed that their Bibles were still sitting on that same shelf next to the kitchen table. I opened Mom's bible to the page held by the pen she used to write notes in the margins and circle passages. The date at the top of the page was September 29th—the day Mom first went to the hospital. Mom had been reading her Bible every day, up until the very day she was no longer able to do so. Mom was storing up Scriptures.

Mom once said in one of her Bible studies: "It's important to make spiritual deposits so that you will be ready for the battles which lie ahead—illness, loss, divorce, broken relationships, etc. It's like storing spiritual fat."[20] Mom had done just that. She had studied and memorized Scriptures throughout her life and had developed a spiritual "fat." And now she found herself desperately depending upon those stored up Scriptures and the truths they held.

I will sing to the Lord all my life;
I will sing praise to my God as long as I live.

Psalm 104:33

Mom had also memorized an abundance of hymns. She had learned to play them on the piano in high school and through the years had found great comfort in their words of faith, hope and God's goodness. They also expressed her thoughts, feelings, and love for the Lord. Although she was no longer able to read a hymnal or play the piano, the words, music and truths spoken through hymns were inscribed on her heart. As she lay in bed and listened to them each day, I am certain that she was singing in her soul.

God's truths and promises were intricately woven into the fabric of Mom's soul and inscribed on her heart. God was preparing her for the day that she would no longer be able to read the Bible for herself or sing her favorite hymns. I fully believe that the power of God's Word ministered to Mom every moment of every hour of every day, especially as she lay trapped in a motionless body. It is my hope and my prayer that one day the bookmark in my own Bible will be placed at the entry of the very day I am no longer able to read it.

God's word is a treasure worth laying up,
and there is no laying it up safely
but in our hearts; if we have it only
in our houses and hands, enemies may
take it from us; if only in our heads,
our memories may fail us: but if our hearts
be delivered into the mold of it,
and the impressions of it remain
on our souls, it is safe.[21]

Love Lifted Me

I was sinking deep in sin, far from the peaceful shore,
Very deeply stained within, sinking to rise no more,
But the Master of the sea, heard my despairing cry,
From the waters lifted me, now safe am I.

Love lifted me! Love lifted me!
When nothing else could help
Love lifted me!

When he saw the wind, he was afraid and,
beginning to sink, cried out, "Lord, save me!"
Immediately Jesus reached out his hand and caught him.

Matthew 14:30-31

15 A Love Story

Day 38

"DIE" Am I going to die? (Because of the severe pain)
"WILL I DIE TODAY"

Our family members returned from the GBS conference today. They were able to visit with one of the leading doctors in GBS research, and he offered to consult on Mom's case and even come visit her. We will send him a copy of her medical records immediately and schedule a time for him to come see Mom.

Day 42

Mom's attention span seems to have narrowed significantly and her ability to communicate to us through raising an eyebrow and moving her lower jaw has also diminished. Since this all began, we have yet to go three days without a significant setback or crisis in her condition. We are now six weeks into this journey, and she continues to show more signs of her condition deteriorating rather than improving. Our greatest struggle at this point is having to watch her continually suffer from the agonizing pain and feelings of helplessness. And that is why we are unbelievably grateful that we serve a God who truly is our "refuge" and our "strength" and our "ever-present help in times of trouble." We have witnessed that so powerfully in the past weeks.

As our bodies become weary and our minds are sometimes confused, our faith in God remains certain and unwavering. It is this faith that has sustained us and will continue to carry us through the difficult days ahead. Please pray for Mom's pain to be controlled (which is a challenge each hour of the day). Please pray for God's miraculous healing of Mom's body—amidst the continued reports of a "very poor prognosis." Please pray for hope, endurance and peace for Mom and for our family. Thank you again for your love and your prayers. We will be forever grateful for each of you and your prayers on our behalf.

Day 45

Today Mom was alert but unable to spell. She appeared to be trying to say something and seemed very frustrated by her inability to communicate. Her pain level was high and required pain med bumps all day. She seemed more at peace when she listened to her music—and especially enjoyed all the loving she received from Dad!

Day 48

Mom enjoyed her time with Dad again today.

"I LUCKY" to have Dad
"WE LUCKY" to have each other
"GIFT" Dad has been her gift.

Now, my God, may your eyes be open and your ears attentive to the prayers offered in this place.

2 Chronicles 6:40

As the days and weeks passed, and as the hope that Mom would recover began to slowly fade, the distress of what we were all experiencing continued to intensify. I could see it especially in the weariness in Dad's face and in the sadness in his eyes. We continued to search for answers, for information, and for hope that Mom might recover, but we were expending all our resources.

My brothers and sisters and I took turns being with Mom throughout her stay in the hospital. Sometimes one or two of us would spend the entire day, and other times we would take turns in the morning, afternoon or evening. But every single day—without exception—Dad stayed for hours at her side. He would sit next to her bed and hold her hand, gently stroking her face, and he would comb his fingers through her hair while quietly talking to her. Even though she was unable to use words, she would speak back to him. He could usually understand what she was trying to say simply by the way she looked at him. He would tell her something and then anticipate her question or response, and Mom would almost always indicate that he was right. And then there were times he would just sit quietly in a chair across the room, watching her as she rested.

"I just didn't get to love you enough." Those were the precious words Mom whispered into Dad's ear as she prepared to be placed on life support weeks earlier. Somehow she knew that those would be the last words she would speak to him, and they were words he grew to cherish. It was very difficult to watch Dad feel so helpless to stop this catastrophic disease that was slowly and painstakingly destroying Mom's body. This man of great faith whose strength and leadership had led our family through so many difficult circumstances for so many years was now powerless to save Mom from her pain and suffering.

Yet through Mom's suffering, we had the privilege to witness the depth of Mom and Dad's love and devotion to each other. His love for her was evident in the way he spoke to her with such affection, the gentle way he stroked her face and kissed her forehead, and his faithful presence by her side—all of which painted for each of us a beautiful picture of their enduring love for one another. Dad told us repeatedly that he wished he were the one lying in that bed instead of Mom. There is no doubt that the sacrificial way he loved her through her suffering brought God glory.

"For this reason a man will leave his father and mother and be united to his wife, and the two will become one flesh. So they are no longer two, but one flesh. Therefore what God has joined together, let no one separate."

Mark 10:7-9

When I told my six year-old daughter that Grandpa wished he could take Grandma's place and be sick instead of her, she responded with a dramatic sigh: "They're such lovebirds!" Yes. Such lovebirds. Their journey of love had begun more than 50 years earlier. They lived a life filled with family, friends, adventures, and joyous occasions. They also held tightly to one another during times of utter heartbreak, intense grief and immense sorrow.

Mom and Dad had the opportunity to celebrate their 50th anniversary just two months before she was stricken by GBS. Dad decided to surprise her with a trip to one of their favorite places, where he presented her with a gift that utterly amazed her—a beautiful diamond ring. Although she was not the least bit surprised at Dad's good taste in jewelry, the fact that he selected it on his own and went to the trouble to surprise her was incredibly meaningful. He also gave her a small photo album filled with old pictures and memories of their years together. They later talked about how much they enjoyed looking at the pictures and discussing all the wonderful experiences they had shared.

Two are better than one, because they have a good return for their labor; If either of them falls down, one can help the other up. But pity anyone who falls and has no one to help them up. Also, if two lie down together, they will keep warm. But how can one keep warm alone? Though one may be overpowered, two can defend themselves. A cord of three strands is not quickly broken.

Ecclesiastes 4:9-12

The cord of three strands symbolizes the strength in a marriage when a husband and wife are joined by God. There have always been three present in my parents' marriage. They continually credited God for helping them through each of the trials they faced and also acknowledged that He was the source of the abundant blessings they had received. Their personal relationships with God had been evident in the foundation of their marriage, and Mom and Dad's love for one another had always been a beautiful reflection of God's love for us. By watching them over the years, I learned a great deal about faithfulness and forgiveness. Like all husbands and wives, they faced challenges in their own lives and in their marriage, but their faith in God and obedience to Him was demonstrated in their commitment and devotion to one another. And throughout Mom's illness, Dad continued to entrust God with the person he loved most in this world.

Husbands, love your wives, just as Christ loved the church and gave himself up for her.

Ephesians 5:25

There is a beautiful grandfather clock in Mom and Dad's living room. Dad had always been careful to wind it in order for the clock to keep the correct time. One evening when Mom was in the hospital, the clock needed to be wound. Someone reached up for the key to do so, but Dad realized what was happening and stopped him: "I am not going to wind the clock—not until Brenda comes home." And so the clock did not get wound that evening, and the time on the clock stood still.

Do you sometimes cry out, as I have,
"God, don't You see my tears? Don't You
see my broken heart? God, never mind
me, but how can You bear to see the agony
of my loved one? God, I know that You
care. I just don't understand why You don't
intervene in this situation right now.
Why don't You do something?
And, God, why did You do that?!"
Then, to my heart, I seem to hear His still,
small voice whispering, "Trust Me.
I know what's best." And I'm left to wonder
why I think I know better than God
what's best for me or my loved one.[22]

Blessed Assurance

Blessed assurance, Jesus is mine!
O what a foretaste of glory divine!
Heir of salvation, purchase of God,
Born of His Spirit, washed in His blood.

This is my story, this is my song,
Praising my Savior, all the day long;
This is my story, this is my song,
Praising my Savior, all the day long.

Let us draw near to God with a sincere heart
and with the full assurance that faith brings.

Hebrews 10:22

---

16 Why I Can Trust Him

"The Lord is my shepherd; I shall not want." Psalm 23:1

Dear friends and family,
With Thanksgiving Day approaching, we remain heartbroken that Mom will not be with us as we gather around the table. We will miss her presence with us, yet we know she would want us to come together and be reminded of our many blessings. Although she continues to have some limited facial movement, she has become noticeably weaker overall. Many times she is unable to focus on what we are saying and is often unresponsive to us when we ask her questions. We continue to pray for a miracle and believe that God is able to perform it. However, we also continue to find comfort as we accept God's will for her life and for our family.

Please pray for strength, relief from pain, and healing for Mom. And please pray for continued patience, strength, wisdom and hope for our family.

Day 52

The specialist whom our family members met at the GBS conference flew in to see Mom. He spent time with her and assessed her condition, and then he met with our family. It was a very difficult meeting. His conclusions were what we had come to expect—but had hoped we would not hear.

His assessment of Mom's condition and prognosis:

- *Mom has a severe form of a rare disorder.*
- *Recovery is expected to be poor and incomplete.*
- *Her quality of life is complicated by the fact that she can perceive everything.*
- *We should expect extreme fluctuation in pain for the rest of her life.*
- *Her nerves "are not there" at this point. They are gone.*
- *She will live life "in a state of dependency."*
- *"There is no realistic hope in the end."*

Day 53

Mom was eager to hear the GBS specialist's prognosis of her condition. Carefully choosing his words, Dad gently explained what he felt she should know. Mom's response:

"BRENDA IS A QUAD" Quadriplegic

Dad tenderly replied: "Yes, for now, that is true."

---

*Trust in the LORD with all your heart
and lean not on your own understanding;
in all your ways submit to him,
and he will make your paths straight.*

Proverbs 3:5-6

Trusting God is a lesson in discipline and commitment. God asks us to trust Him with our own lives and the lives of our loved ones.

He asks us to trust Him with our burdens and give our worries to Him. He asks us to give Him the authority over our lives and believe that He will care for us and provide our every need. He asks us to have faith that He is working all things together for good if we will love Him. But why *can* we trust Him? Why *should* we trust Him? I began to think about the character of God and my relationship with Him, and that led me to some of the answers to these questions.

For you created my inmost being; you knit me together in my mother's womb. I praise you because I am fearfully and wonderfully made.

Psalm 139:13

So God created mankind in his own image, in the image of God he created them; male and female he created them.

Genesis 1:27

God created me. The God of the universe created me in His own image, and I am "fearfully and wonderfully made." Why would God create me out of His expansive love and in His own image and then want to harm me? I love my own children so deeply. They are my treasured possessions. When I establish rules, provide discipline or offer direction, they don't always feel that I have their best interest at heart, but I do. Likewise, I am a child of God. He is the Father with perfect wisdom and discernment and knows what is best for me, not necessarily what I think should happen or what feels good to me, but what He knows I need. I am God's wonderful creation and His child. That is one reason I can trust Him.

"For I know the plans I have for you," declares the LORD,
"plans to prosper you and not to harm you,
plans to give you hope and a future."

Jeremiah 29:11

God has a plan for me. God is all-knowing, all-powerful, and ever-present. He sees everything that has happened in my life and everything that is to come. He has a plan for my life, and it is a perfect plan. I may not like or desire certain events or circumstances that occur, and I may not welcome the pain that I must endure, but God is sovereign and is not going to allow anything to happen to me for which He has not prepared me. Because He knows everything that will happen before it transpires, I can have the faith and confidence that God has fully equipped me and will take care of me through life's adversities. God has a plan for my life, and I can trust that plan and trust Him.

He was despised and rejected by mankind, a man of suffering, and
familiar with pain. Like one from whom people hide their faces
he was despised, and we held him in low esteem. Surely he took up
our pain and bore our suffering, yet we considered him punished
by God, stricken by him, and afflicted. But he was pierced for our
transgressions, he was crushed for our iniquities; the punishment that
brought us peace was on him, and by his wounds we are healed.

Isaiah 53:3-5

He knows my suffering. God revealed Himself to mankind through Jesus, His Son, and Jesus experienced terrible pain and suffering. He was despised and rejected. He suffered emotionally, psychologically and physically. I have a God who knows pain and suffering—not only His suffering through Jesus, but His suffering as a Father who watched His Son experience a horribly painful death. Therefore, I have a God of compassion who knows fully what I need in my own time of suffering.

God promises to provide for my every need. He does not promise that He will give me the strength to do only *some* things. He doesn't promise to provide *most* of my needs. He promises to provide *all* of my needs. He is my "ever-present help in times of trouble" (Psalm 46:1). Only the God of the universe and the Creator of all things has the power and ability to provide my every need at all times. As much as I love my children, I am unable and ill-equipped to provide their every need in all circumstances, but I have a God who promises to do just that—not only for me—but also for those I love.

This is how God showed his love among us: He sent his one and only Son into the world that we might live through him. This is love: not that we loved God, but that he loved us and sent his Son as an atoning sacrifice for our sins.

1 John 4:9-10

He loves me. He loves me not because I love Him. He loved me first even though I am a sinner. He loves me when I am not faithful and when I doubt and question Him. He loves me, and His love is perfect and unwavering. His love endures forever—for all of eternity. No one's love is greater for me than God's. His love for me is so great that He sent His perfect and sinless Son to suffer and die for my sins. God desires a personal relationship with me, and He knew that the only way to accomplish that was for Jesus to die on the cross. That is how much He loves me, and that is why I can trust Him.

We must cease striving and trust God
to provide what He thinks is best
and in whatever time He chooses
to make it available.
But this kind of trusting
doesn't come naturally. It's a spiritual
crisis of the will in which we must choose
to exercise faith.[23]

When I think of why I can trust God, I am reminded of His character and His love for me and for all of His children. He created each of us in His own image and has a plan for our lives. He understands our suffering and knows exactly what we need to get through every trial and difficulty we will endure. He loves us. As much as I loved my mom, I know that God's love for her was unlimited and unfathomable, and so I chose to trust Him with her life.

Would someone who loves you so deeply
love you poorly? You can trust Him.[24]

Because of the Lord's great love we are not consumed,
for his compassions never fail. They are new every morning;
great is your faithfulness.
Lamentations 3:22-23

Standing on the Promises

Standing on the promises of Christ my King,
Through eternal ages let His praises ring,
Glory in the highest, I will shout and sing,
Standing on the promises of God.

Standing, standing,
Standing on the promises of God my Savior;
Standing, standing,
I'm standing on the promises of God.

My eyes stay open through the watches of the night,
that I may meditate on your promises.

Psalm 119:148

---

17 God's Promises Fill Me Up

Day 55 - Thanksgiving Day

Mom asked to listen to her hymns a lot today. It has been a very sad day for all of us. We had bought some Christmas decorations for Mom's room, but she was so sad—and so were we—so we didn't want to emphasize Christmas right now. At this time we are uncertain as to what the future holds.

Day 56 – Morning

"NIGHTMARE"

"HOSPITAL ON FIRE"

"I AM STILL HAVING SIDE EFFECTS FROM THE PAIN MEDS"

Mom said she was scared, and that she is very sad. She did not sleep well. The medication is likely giving her terrifying nightmares and hallucinations, and she is having an extremely difficult time communicating her thoughts to us. It's frustrating for her and heartbreaking for us. At one point, the nurse tried to place an eye patch on Mom to help relieve the pain she was experiencing in one of her eyes. She was noticeably distraught and spelled:

"CALL DAD"

"NO PATCH"

She wanted us to ask Dad:

"WHAT ABOUT THE PATCH"

Mom had heard Dad say earlier that he was uncertain that he wanted them to put a patch on her eye, but he reassured her it was okay, and she allowed the nurse to proceed.

"Come to me, all you who are weary and burdened, and I will give you rest. Take my yoke upon you and learn from me, for I am gentle and humble in heart, and you will find rest for your souls. For my yoke is easy and my burden is light."

Matthew 11:28

Gathering around Mom's table for Thanksgiving lunch without her present was very difficult for our family. Several of us spent the morning at the hospital before returning home for lunch, while others stayed with her throughout the afternoon. Although we worked hard to prepare the meal just as she would have instructed and made every effort to celebrate the day, our hearts were heavy. There was a dark cloud of sadness that had descended upon the day that never seemed to dissipate.

We felt incredibly helpless. We had spent countless hours at Mom's bedside, holding her hand, and telling her how much we loved her. All we could do was tend to her expressed needs at the time when she was feeling hot, cold, in need of more pain medication, or to be turned over in an attempt to alleviate the pain. At times she could spell out her needs or thoughts to us, but more often she would grow too tired to finish a word or sentence. Her eyes were often filled with expressions of helplessness and desperation, to which we could only respond: "We are so sorry, Mom. We love you so much."

We began to accept the reality that Mom was not going to get better. The disease was not going to reverse, and her ability to live independently of life support was not going to be possible. The hope that a miracle would come had gradually faded, and we were having to face the unimaginable decision of withdrawing Mom's life support as she had been asking us to do for weeks. God knew that we hadn't been prepared to make that decision, but now that was changing. As the reality of Mom's condition became clear and our hope for a different outcome melted away, we depended upon God—more than ever—to lead us and grant us wisdom.

The LORD *is the everlasting God,*
the Creator of the ends of the earth.
He will not grow tired or weary,
and his understanding no one can fathom.
He gives strength to the weary
and increases the power of the weak.
Even youths grow tired and weary,
and young men stumble and fall;
but those who hope in the Lord
will renew their strength.
They will soar on wings like eagles;
they will run and not grow weary,
they will walk and not be faint.

Isaiah 40:28-31

One afternoon I looked out into my parents' back yard at their swimming pool. I thought of how the water in a pool is constantly being drained, yet its water level is consistent because the jets on the sides of the pool are continuously adding more water. I sometimes feel like I am in a pool with a drain at the bottom—and my strength and hope are gradually being depleted. Yet I realize that God is constantly sustaining me to keep my heart and spirit filled. I know that I cannot stop the despair and burdens of life from draining me, but I can always rely upon God's promise that "He will not grow tired or weary" and that He will renew my strength.

> *Our faith keeps us from being*
> *swallowed up by despair*
> *but I don't think it makes*
> *our loss hurt any less.*[25]

One of the ways that God strengthens me is through His promises in Scripture—His powerful reminders of His ability and desire to sustain me in times of difficulty. Just as one holds a lamp to light a path in the darkness, the light in my hand is the hope of those promises. I often struggle to see what is in the distance or where I am headed, but God can see over every mountain and around every corner. He sees through the blinding darkness because He is the light that dissolves it. Therefore, I can trust Him to guide me, and when necessary, to carry me.

And so each day I experienced the promises of God amidst the pain and suffering. He used the chaos and turmoil to manifest Himself in my life, to perfect my faith, and to remind me of my unending need for Him. As my heart would become drained of hope, He would once again fill my soul with His promises.

"I have told you these things, so that in me you may have peace.
In this world you will have trouble. But take heart!
I have overcome the world."

John 16:33

He has delivered us from such a deadly peril,
and he will deliver us. On him we have set our hope
that he will continue to deliver us.

2 Corinthians 1:10

But I will sing of your strength, in the morning
I will sing of your love; for you are my fortress,
my refuge in times of trouble.

Psalm 59:16

"Because he loves me," says the Lord, "I will rescue him;
I will protect him, for he acknowledges my name.
He will call on me, and I will answer him;
I will be with him in trouble."

Psalm 91:15-16

Cast all your anxiety on him because he cares for you.

1 Peter 5: 7

Let the morning bring me word of your unfailing love,
for I have put my trust in you. Show me the way I should go,
for to you I entrust my life.

Psalm 143:8

Let all that I am praise the Lord;
may I never forget the good things he does for me.

Psalm 103:2 NLT

Do not be anxious about anything, but in every situation, by prayer
and petition, with thanksgiving, present your requests to God. And
the peace of God, which transcends all understanding, will guard
your hearts and your minds in Christ Jesus.

Philippians 4:6-7

I Surrender All

All to Jesus, I surrender;
All to Him I freely give;
I will ever love and trust Him,
In His presence daily live.

I surrender all, I surrender all,
All to Thee, my blessed Savior,
I surrender all.

"In the same way, those of you who do not give up
everything you have cannot be my disciples."

Luke 14:33

---

18 Gaining God's Perspective

Day 56 - Evening

"Give thanks to the Lord, for He is good; His love endures forever"
1 Chronicles 16:34

From Dad:

Even in these trying times for us, we have much to be thankful for. We are especially grateful to each of you for your love, prayers and support. Brenda's condition has not changed in the past several weeks. One of the leading experts on GBS came to visit her and our family. He confirmed the very disturbing prognosis we were given by each of the doctors who have seen her. While I am saddened by Brenda's condition, I am very thankful for the support of our family and friends. As you continue to pray for Brenda, please also pray for our family.

Carey

Day 57

"PLEASE TELL THEM TO LET ME GO."

Day 60

"JOYOUS" Mom told us to be joyous.
That was the last word Mom spelled.

Mom had continued to ask for us to let her go. She was ready. She had been ready. She knew that she would finally be freed from pain, and she knew well the heavenly homecoming that awaited her. Mom had made her wishes completely clear—not only since being in the hospital—but she had told her friends and family many, many times over the years that she never wanted to live in a state of dependency. We had always known that, and we had constantly reassured her we would not allow her to live that way, but we just kept trying to believe in a miracle that never happened. I fully believed God's promise of healing and restoration for her—I just didn't know if it would be on this side of Heaven or when she arrived in the arms of Jesus.

> *There are times when the will of God*
> *is hard to discern and easy to do,*
> *times when it is easy to discern*
> *and hard to do, and other times*
> *when it is hard to discern and hard to do.*
> *That last one is where I am.*[26]

Sometimes the will of God truly is difficult to discern and even more difficult to do. We were faced with the most heart-wrenching decision of our lives, but God had prepared our hearts to make it with grace, wisdom, discernment and clarity. We are a large family filled with varying and strong personalities. Dad had continued to tell us that if we were going to have to make the decision to withdraw Mom's life support that God would give each of us a peace and clarity regarding that decision. We had each traveled different journeys, but in the grip of inexplicable sorrow, we had arrived at the same conclusion. Mom did not want to live that way. She wanted us to let her go.

There was nothing left to do but grant her wishes and extend the grace to her that I know she would have granted to any of us if we had been in her place. I didn't want to keep Mom on life support for my own selfish reasons, but I could hardly bear the thought of her really being gone. Even though she was unable to speak, she was still present, and I could be with her, sit with her, and occasionally understand what she was attempting to communicate. But her pain was so excruciating, and her psychological suffering was so unimaginable. I knew the merciful decision would be to grant her request and allow her to be free from the pain and sorrow. I knew that granting that wish would leave us without her, but it would also allow her to finally experience complete freedom and healing. Her heart's desire was to be released into the arms of her Savior. She had long ago surrendered her heart and mind to Jesus and had accepted God's will for her life. It was now our turn to surrender all.

I waited patiently for the LORD; he turned to me and heard my cry.
He lifted me out of the slimy pit, out of the mud and mire;
he set my feet on a rock and gave me a firm place to stand.
He put a new song in my mouth, a hymn of praise to our God.
Many will see and fear the LORD and put their trust in him.

Psalm 40:1-3

Joseph's brothers couldn't understand why Joseph did not punish them for selling him into slavery decades earlier. Nebuchadnezzar couldn't understand why Shadrach, Meshach and Abednego refused to bow down to him, and instead, were willingly thrown into a fiery furnace. The criminal next to Jesus on the cross couldn't understand why Jesus refused to save himself. God had a different perspective than each of these people, and the events in their lives transpired in order for God's purposes to be accomplished and His glory be more fully revealed.

The Lord does not look at the things people look at.
People look at the outward appearance,
but the Lord looks at the heart.

1 Samuel 16:7

I often look at life from my own limited perspective, failing to understand God's perspective, His purpose, and His plan. Our family did not fully understand why we had to experience the horror of the past 60 days, but we had repeatedly seen God's glory revealed and knew that the ultimate purpose was for that to be accomplished. From a medical perspective, we were finally prepared to accept that there is "no realistic hope in the end." But we also knew that from an eternal perspective, God's perspective, there is *extraordinary* hope in the end.

I've read the last page of the Bible,
it's all going to turn out all right.[27]

We made the decision that we would honor Mom's wishes and withdraw life support at 10 am the following morning. The ladies in her beloved Bible study were already scheduled to meet and pray for her at that time. It would also be the first day of December—her absolute favorite month of the year—the month in which she was born, and more importantly, the month in which she celebrated the birth of her Savior.

In the midst of our heartbreak, God had affirmed our decision and granted us an unexplainable peace that we were making the right decision at the right time. Letting Mom go was the ultimate act of obedience to what we believed God was calling us to do—to fully and finally surrender Mom to Him.

Peace I leave with you; my peace I give you.
I do not give to you as the world gives.
Do not let your hearts be troubled and do not be afraid.

John 14:27

Softly and Tenderly Jesus Is Calling

Softly and tenderly Jesus is calling,
Calling for you and for me;
See, on the portals He's waiting and watching,
Watching for you and for me.

Come home, come home,
You who are weary, come home;
Earnestly, tenderly, Jesus is calling,
Calling, O sinner, come home!

He calls his own sheep by name and leads them out.

John 10:3

19 The Last and Greatest Lesson

Today we are brokenhearted. Our spirits are crushed. Our precious Mom has gone home. Mom was unable to survive complications from a catastrophic and irreversible case of Guillain-Barré Syndrome. The doctors who have cared for Mom and the two GBS experts who have seen her made it clear that she is among only 2% of all GBS patients who suffer from an incredibly rare form of the disease and that she would not recover. Knowing that, we have honored the wishes which Mom has expressed to each of us repeatedly and let her go to be with God. Mom bravely fought this battle for the past 60 days, and in her final moments she was surrounded by her family—who absolutely adored her!

Although we are overcome with sadness, we have been greatly comforted by the way our precious Dad—whose loss is even greater than ours—has led us through our family's darkest hours with unwavering faith, courage and love. Dad's gentle, tender affection and unconditional love for Mom over these past weeks will forever be etched in our hearts.

We are also comforted to know she is now fully and miraculously healed in the presence of her Lord and Savior, and we believe that God was standing at the pearly gates with His arms open wide as He welcomed her home.

The Lord is close to the brokenhearted
and saves those who are crushed in spirit.

Psalm 34:18

The drive that morning was the most difficult I have ever taken. The day was December 1st. It was the first day of Mom's favorite month of the year. It was the month in which she was born and the month in which she was returning home to the One who gave her life. The decision to withdraw Mom's life support was mixed with peace and grief, hope and sadness, as well as certainty and despair. God had provided each of us with the peace and strength to grant Mom's clearly and consistently expressed desires for her life. It was our final act of selfless love for her.

When we arrived at the critical care unit that morning, the nurses and doctors were aware of the situation and incredibly sensitive to our circumstances. There were few words spoken but so much compassion expressed. The attending physician's sensitivity, kindness and leadership were further expressions of God's enduring grace to our family. Mom was heavily sedated that morning, but as we each took a turn to say goodbye, several of us felt that she was aware of what was to happen and the decision being made on her behalf. The song "We are Standing on Holy Ground" played quietly in the room, and we knew that God's angels truly were all around. Finally, we gathered around her bed as we held hands and released her into the loving arms of her Heavenly Father—to whom she had always belonged.

*Jesus said, "For I have come down from heaven
not to do my will but to do the will of him who sent me."*

John 6:38

Mom surrendered her life to Jesus as a child and spent the rest of her life wanting to be like him. Mom never wavered in her pursuit of God and her effort to grow in her relationship with Christ. She regularly attended and served at her church, shared her faith with others, and diligently studied the Bible. She strived to show love, compassion and grace to those whom she loved and to those whom she had just met. If you had asked Mom, "What would you do for God?" she would most certainly have replied, "Anything." Yet none of the trials and adversities Mom had faced in her life could compare to the 60 days she suffered from such an extremely rare, excruciatingly painful, and totally devastating disease.

I have come to believe that Mom's sincere desire to be Christ-like is what led to her suffering in her last days. She knew that surrendering her life to the Lord would require much—she just didn't know how much. Although she was far from perfect, Mom had done nothing to deserve such agonizing emotional, mental and physical pain. But God knew that Mom desired for Him to use her life to fulfill His purposes—all for His glory. God's love for Mom was unwavering and immeasurable, and what happened in her life was not apart from that love but because she was immersed in it.

*No matter how deep our darkness,
He is deeper still.*[28]

God had been equipping Mom for this battle and had been preparing her testimony for others to witness as they watched, prayed and anticipated the outcome of her illness. On the day Mom died, there had been more than 24,000 visits to her CaringBridge website and more than 1,250 messages written to her and our family. There were people praying across the country, and across the world, for her and for us. Her witness and the power of her testimony in life—and now in death—were extraordinary.

Several years earlier, Mom had written a Bible study entitled "Why?" The powerful words she wrote in that lesson revealed the depths of her faith and the trust she had in God's plan for her life:

> *Everything we go through has a purpose.*
> *All our pains and miseries—our struggles,*
> *our heartaches and our hassles are for one*
> *purpose—a chance for us to glorify God.*
> *God may have selected us to suffer through*
> *something, so that we can give Him the*
> *glory. He has higher plans for us than*
> *just the tragedy we are enduring. God's*
> *glory can be displayed in so many ways—*
> *the heavens and stars, people and their*
> *problems, the majesty of the mountains,*
> *the ebb and flow of the oceans.*
> *But nothing is so amazing and so*
> *remarkable as proclaiming God's glory*
> *amidst our problems.*[29]

Mom's depth of faith was the hallmark of her life and most definitely her legacy. Her ultimate goal in life was to be Christ-like in all she did, even though she would be the first to tell you that she fell short in many ways. The desire of Mom's heart was to bring God glory and to be obedient to His calling in her life—even when that included physical suffering—and ultimately her own death.

And they have defeated him by the blood of the Lamb and by their testimony. And they did not love their lives so much that they were afraid to die.

Revelation 12:11 NLT

What Mom taught me about love, friendship, family, hospitality and faith have greatly influenced and molded my life and the person I am today. She taught me to laugh and to celebrate the small and great accomplishments in life. She taught me to worry less about doing things perfectly and to enjoy doing them. She showed me how to love my kids well and the importance of allowing them to play in the rain and roll in the sand. She taught me to believe in the beauty, wonder and miracle of Christmas. She taught me that a home is not meant to be perfect but meant to be shared. She taught me that God gives us blessings, so that we can share them with others. She taught me that I don't have to be perfect to represent Jesus to those God places in my path. She taught me to give generously and love extravagantly. Mom taught me what really matters in life.

Nevertheless, each person should live as a believer in whatever situation the Lord has assigned to them, just as God has called them.

1 Corinthians 7:17

The many lessons I have learned from my mom throughout my life have profoundly impacted me, but her final act of surrendering her life fully and completely to the Lord has been the greatest lesson of all. To whom much is given, much is expected, and she clearly demonstrated the depth of her faith in God and His calling in her life. Mom faithfully and obediently poured out all she had been given, and she accomplished all that had been assigned to her by God. Her work on earth was finally done.

I have fought the good fight, I have finished the race,
I have kept the faith.

2 Timothy 4:7

How Great Thou Art

O Lord my God! When I in awesome wonder
Consider all the worlds Thy hands have made,
I see the stars, I hear the rolling thunder,
Thy power throughout the universe displayed,

Then sings my soul, my Saviour God to Thee;
How great Thou art, how great Thou art!

When Christ shall come with shout of acclamation
And take me home, what joy shall fill my heart!
Then I shall bow in humble adoration
And there proclaim, my God, how great Thou art!

Great is the Lord and most worthy of praise.

Psalm 145:3

20 A Prism of Light

Life is filled with heartache. Only God can fully comprehend the depth of grief and the severity of sorrow that is endured by each of us. For those who have experienced the pain of a broken heart, we know that there will be more because we live in a fallen, sinful world, but we can also be assured that God will continue to carry us in His strong, loving arms.

As I reflect on my family's journey through the darkness of those 60 days, I am reminded of the many ways in which God's sovereignty, glory and character were illuminated. The light of His love was continually revealed through His unending grace, life-giving hope, and promise of eternal life through Jesus Christ. That light was further evident through the love of my own family, those who prayed for us and cared for us, and through my mom's enduring trust and faith in her Lord and Savior.

Dad once said: "Brenda was special, and the thing that made her special is that she had no idea she was special. In her mind, everyone was special." And that is, indeed, how Mom treated everyone. It didn't matter who you were, what you had accomplished, or what had transpired in your past. She accepted you, loved you, and shined God's love into your life.

One day when I was sitting next to Mom in the hospital, God brought to my mind a prism. I was reminded of how a prism takes what appears to be white, colorless light and breaks it up to spray forth all the colors of the rainbow. I realized that Mom did the same with God's love. She was simply a prism through which

God's light bursts forth to others—shining all the colors of the rainbow into our lives. Yet she would have most certainly said that anything good and any beauty you saw in her were simply God's light shining through her.

Mom's Prism of Love
by Cindy Janecka

God's love poured down from Heaven
shining brightly through Mom's life
in a rainbow of majestic colors
bursting forth in glorious light.

Just as a prism takes white light
and breaks it into a spectrum of colors,
Mom took God's unfailing love
and found ways to share it with others.

We've all been blessed by Mom
in ways beyond measure and belief.
She's done so much for each of us
and given us more love than we could keep.

So, Lord, show us how to share Your love
by also making our lives a prism,
reflecting the amazing love that You—
through Mom—to us have given.[30]

Even after everything she experienced, I have no doubt that Mom would want us to give God glory with our own lives in all circumstances. She would also want us to experience the love and saving grace of Jesus and share it with others and allow our lives to become a prism through which God casts His light into the lives of those around us.

At Mom's memorial service, the church was filled with nearly 1,500 people, all whose lives were in some way impacted by her. As part of her eulogy, one of my sisters asked everyone present who had shared a meal at Mom's table to please stand, and from the front of the church, there was not one visible person still sitting. The memorial service celebrated the life Mom lived, the lives she touched, and the legacy she left behind. And most importantly, God was truly glorified through the commemoration of her life. She would have been very pleased.

Later that evening the commotion of the day had finally subsided, and there were only a few of us left at Dad's house. As the sun began to set on a very long day, I watched as Dad quietly got up from the chair where he was seated, walked over and wound the grandfather clock. Mom was finally home.

Amazing Grace

Amazing grace! How sweet the sound,
That saved a wretch like me!
I once was lost, but now am found;
Was blind, but now I see.

The Lord has promised good to me;
His Word my hope secures;
He will my Shield and Portion be,
As long as life endures.

When we've been there ten thousand years,
Bright shining as the sun,
We've no less days to sing God's praise
Than when we'd first begun.

For it is by grace you have been saved, through faith—
and this is not from yourselves, it is the gift of God.

Ephesians 2:8

Epilogue

When this journey began, Mom knew she would not be coming home to us. She told us that as we waited for the ambulance the morning she woke up and was unable to walk. Later that evening, just moments before she was placed on life support and in a medically induced coma, the words she spoke to each of us as we gathered around her bedside also made that very clear. Although Mom was prepared to go to Heaven, she was unaware that she would have to endure two excruciating months of suffering to get there, but God did.

Mom's pleas of "let me go" were heartbreaking, but we had to pursue every possibility that she could overcome the devastation of that disease. She patiently waited for us to exhaust every recommended treatment, research every medical study available, and consult multiple GBS specialists—until we conceded that she was right.

God provided us the courage and strength to finally accept what Mom desired for her life. One of her doctors reminded us that we were not making the decision for her but instead communicating on her behalf what we knew to be her wishes. Each of us were confident that our decision to withdraw her life support was exactly what she had been pleading for, but we also knew it would be a controversial decision and one with which some people would disagree. However, it was our responsibility to honor Mom and her will for her own life—which she had made abundantly clear. It was only through exhaustive prayer and relentlessly seeking God's direction that He led us to trust and accept what we believed to be His will for her life.

As Mom's life on earth came to an end, our grieving began. Grieving can be hard and tiring. I have spent a great deal of time reflecting over the painful journey that filled those two months, and words still seem inadequate to describe the impact that experience has had on my life. I have tried to let the heartwarming memories of Mom outshine the heartache of seeing her suffer and losing her, but the healing of a broken heart takes time.

Our family has carried on many of the traditions which Mom began—Dad's formal birthday dinner, celebrating the "Twelve Days of Christmas," gathering for her birthday breakfast every Christmas Eve, enjoying summer vacations in Galveston and snow-filled ski trips to Colorado, inviting friends to enjoy holiday meals, and delighting in the celebrations of birthdays and other milestones of the grandkids. I now teach the Bible study in Mom's place, and I understand why she considered it such a privilege to study God's word and to share His truths with the ladies in our group.

Since Mom died, one of the greatest blessings that has transpired in my own life has been my deepened friendship with my dad. I have had the opportunity to learn so much more about him and share my life with him in ways I had never done before. He has truly become one of my best friends.

As the years go by, the impact of Mom's life on my own has not diminished. Her infectious joy, her love of life, and her profound faith infiltrate so many aspects of my life and are still vivid in my mind. I will forever treasure each of those memories and look forward to being reunited with her in Heaven—and what a day of rejoicing that will be!

Guillain-Barré Syndrome

The following information is taken from the website of the National Institute of Neurological Disorders and Stroke. www.ninds.nih.gov/disorders/gbs/detail_gbs.htm

What is Guillain-Barré Syndrome?

Guillain-Barré syndrome (GBS) is a disorder in which the body's immune system attacks part of the peripheral nervous system. The first symptoms of this disorder include varying degrees of weakness or tingling sensations in the legs. In many instances the symmetrical weakness and abnormal sensations spread to the arms and upper body. These symptoms can increase in intensity until certain muscles cannot be used at all and, when severe, the person is almost totally paralyzed. In these cases the disorder is life threatening - potentially interfering with breathing and, at times, with blood pressure or heart rate - and is considered a medical emergency. Such an individual is often put on a ventilator to assist with breathing and is watched closely for problems such as an abnormal heart beat, infections, blood clots, and high or low blood pressure. Most individuals, however, have good recovery from even the most severe cases of Guillain-Barré syndrome, although some continue to have a certain degree of weakness.

Guillain-Barré syndrome can affect anybody. It can strike at any age, and both sexes are equally prone to the disorder. The syndrome is rare, however, afflicting only about one person in 100,000. Usually Guillain-Barré occurs a few days or weeks after the patient has had symptoms of a respiratory or gastrointestinal viral infection.

Occasionally surgery will trigger the syndrome. In rare instances vaccinations may increase the risk of GBS.

After the first clinical manifestations of the disease, the symptoms can progress over the course of hours, days or weeks. Most people reach the stage of greatest weakness within the first 2 weeks after symptoms appear, and by the third week of the illness 90 percent of all patients are at their weakest.

What causes Guillain-Barré syndrome?

No one yet knows why Guillain-Barré—which is not contagious—strikes some people and not others. Nor does anyone know exactly what sets the disease in motion.

What scientists do know is that the body's immune system begins to attack the body itself, causing what is known as an autoimmune disease. Usually the cells of the immune system attack only foreign material and invading organisms. In Guillain-Barré syndrome, however, the immune system starts to destroy the myelin sheath that surrounds the axons of many peripheral nerves, or even the axons themselves (axons are long, thin extensions of the nerve cells; they carry nerve signals). The myelin sheath surrounding the axon speeds up the transmission of nerve signals and allows the transmission of signals over long distances.

In diseases in which the peripheral nerves' myelin sheaths are injured or degraded, the nerves cannot transmit signals efficiently. That is why the muscles begin to lose their ability to respond to the brain's commands, commands that must be carried through the nerve network. The brain also receives fewer sensory signals from the rest of the body, resulting in an inability to feel textures, heat, pain and other sensations. Alternately, the brain may receive inappropriate signals that result in tingling, "crawling-skin," or painful sensations. Because the signals to and from the arms and legs must travel the longest distances they are most vulnerable to interruption. Therefore, muscle weakness and tingling sensations usually first appear in the hands and feet and progress upwards.

When Guillain-Barré is preceded by a viral or bacterial infection, it is possible that the virus has changed the nature of cells in the nervous system so that the immune system treats them as foreign cells. It is also possible that the virus makes the immune system itself less discriminating about what cells it recognizes as its own, allowing some of the immune cells, such as certain kinds of lymphocytes and macrophages, to attack the myelin. Sensitized T lymphocytes cooperate with B lymphocytes to produce antibodies against components of the myelin sheath and may contribute to destruction of the myelin. In two forms of GBS, axons are attacked by antibodies against the bacteria Campylobacter jejuni, which react with proteins of the peripheral nerves. Acute motor axonal neuropathy is particularly common in Chinese children. Scientists are investigating these and other possibilities to find why the immune system goes awry in Guillain-Barré syndrome and other autoimmune diseases. The cause and course of Guillain-Barré syndrome is an active area of neurological investigation, incorporating the cooperative efforts of neurological scientists, immunologists and virologists.

How is Guillain-Barré syndrome diagnosed?

Guillain-Barré is called a syndrome rather than a disease because it is not clear that a specific disease-causing agent is involved. A syndrome is a medical condition characterized by a collection of symptoms (what the patient feels) and signs (what a doctor can observe or measure). The signs and symptoms of the syndrome can be quite varied, so doctors may, on rare occasions, find it difficult to diagnose Guillain-Barré in its earliest stages.

Where can I get more information?

GBS/CIDP Foundation International
The Holly Building 104 1/2 Forrest Ave.
Narberth, PA 19072
info@gbs-cidp.org
http://www.gbs-cidp.org
610-667-0131
866-224-3301

Scriptures

So do not fear, for I am with you; do not be dismayed,
for I am your God. I will strengthen you and help you;
I will uphold you with my righteous right hand.
Isaiah 41:10

"I am the Alpha and the Omega," says the Lord God,
"who is, and who was, and who is to come, the Almighty."
Revelation 1:8

Be strong and courageous.
Do not be afraid or terrified because of them,
for the Lord your God goes with you;
he will never leave you nor forsake you.
Deuteronomy 31:6

Be joyful in hope, patient in affliction, faithful in prayer.
Romans 12:12

He will have no fear of bad news; his heart is steadfast,
trusting in the Lord. His heart is steady, he will not be afraid,
until he looks in triumph on his adversaries.
Psalm 112:7-8

[Job] replied: "You are talking like a foolish woman.
Shall we accept good from God, and not trouble?"
Job 2:10

But we also glory in our sufferings,
because we know that suffering produces perseverance;
perseverance, character; and character, hope.

Romans 5:3-4

My God is my rock, in whom I take refuge,
my shield and the horn of my salvation.
He is my stronghold, my refuge and my savior.

2 Samuel 22:3

The Lord Almighty has sworn, "Surely, as I have planned,
so it will be, and as I have purposed, so it will stand."

Isaiah 14:24

...so that no one would be unsettled by these trials.
For you know quite well that we are destined for them.

1 Thessalonians 3:3

Now faith is being sure of what we hope for
and certain of what we do not see.

Hebrews 11:1

Share with the Lord's people who are in need.
Practice hospitality.

Romans 12:13

Cheerfully share your home with those who need a meal or a place
to stay. God has given each of you a gift from his great variety of
spiritual gifts. Use them well to serve one another.

1 Peter 4:9-10 NLT

But in your hearts revere Christ as Lord. Always be prepared
to give an answer to everyone who asks you to give the reason
for the hope that you have but do this with gentleness and respect.

1 Peter 3:15

And whatever you do, whether in word or deed,
do it all in the name of the Lord Jesus,
giving thanks to God the Father through him.
Colossians 3:17

Charm is deceptive, and beauty does not last;
but a woman who fears the Lord will be greatly praised.
Reward her for all she has done.
Let her deeds publicly declare her praise.
Proverbs 30:30-31

Now if we are children, then we are heirs—heirs of God
and co-heirs with Christ, if indeed we share in his sufferings
in order that we may also share in his glory.
Romans 8:17

"When you pass through the waters, I will be with you;
and when you pass through the rivers, they will not sweep over you.
When you walk through the fire, you will not be burned;
the flames will not set you ablaze. For I am the Lord, your God,
the Holy One of Israel, your Savior; Do not be afraid,
for I am with you."
Isaiah 43:2-3, 5

God is our refuge and strength, an ever-present help in trouble.
Therefore we will not fear, though the earth give way and the
mountains fall into the heart of the sea, though its waters roar and
foam and the mountains quake with their surging.
Psalm 46:1-3

"…everyone who is called by my name,
whom I created for my glory, whom I formed and made."
Isaiah 43:7

Now a man named Lazarus was sick. He was from Bethany,
the village of Mary and her sister Martha. (This Mary, whose brother
Lazarus now lay sick, was the same one who poured perfume
on the Lord and wiped his feet with her hair.) So the sisters sent
word to Jesus, "Lord, the one you love is sick." When he heard this,
Jesus said, "This sickness will not end in death. No, it is for God's
glory so that God's Son may be glorified through it." Now Jesus
loved Martha and her sister and Lazarus. So when he heard that
Lazarus was sick, he stayed where he was two more days, and then
he said to his disciples, "Let us go back to Judea."
John 11:1-4

They will see his face, and his name will be on their foreheads.
There will be no more night. They will not need the light of a lamp
or the light of the sun, for the Lord God will give them light.
And they will reign for ever and ever.
Revelation 22:3-4

Therefore we do not lose heart. Though outwardly we are
wasting away, yet inwardly we are being renewed day by day.
For our light and momentary troubles are achieving for us
an eternal glory that far outweighs them all.
2 Corinthians 4:16-17

He reveals deep and hidden things;
he knows what lies in darkness, and light dwells with him.
Daniel 2:22

And we know that in all things God works for the good of those who
love him, who have been called according to his purpose.
Romans 8:28

Rather, as servants of God we commend ourselves in every way:
in great endurance; in troubles, hardships and distresses.
2 Corinthians 6:4

The Lord works out everything for his own ends—
even the wicked for a day of disaster. In his heart a man plans
his course, but the Lord determines his steps.
Proverbs 16:4,9

For we are God's masterpiece. He has created us anew in Christ Jesus,
so we can do the good things he planned for us long ago.
Ephesians 2:10 NLT

Many are the plans in a man's heart,
but it is the Lord's purpose that prevails.
Proverbs 19:21

I lift up my eyes to the hills—where does my help come from? My help
comes from the Lord, the Maker of heaven and earth. He will not let
your foot slip—he who watches over you will not slumber; indeed,
he who watches over Israel will neither slumber nor sleep. The Lord
watches over you; the Lord is your shade at your right hand; the sun
will not harm you by day, nor the moon by night. The Lord will keep
you from all harm—he will watch over your life; the Lord will watch
over your coming and going both now and forevermore.
Psalm 121

He heals the brokenhearted and binds up their wounds.
Psalm 147:3

The righteous cry out, and the Lord hears them;
he delivers them from all their troubles.
Psalm 34:17

Praise be to the God and Father of our Lord Jesus Christ,
the Father of compassion and the God of all comfort,
who comforts us in all our troubles, so that we can comfort those
in any trouble with the comfort we ourselves receive from God.
2 Corinthians 1:3-4

Find rest, O my soul, in God alone. My hope comes from Him.
He alone is my rock and my salvation. He is my fortress.
I will not be shaken.
Psalm 62:5-6

Lord, hear my prayer, listen to my cry for mercy;
in your faithfulness and righteousness come to my relief.
Psalm 143:8-11

And this same God who takes care of me
will supply all your needs from his glorious riches,
which have been given to us in Christ Jesus.
Philippians 4:19 NLT

"The mountains be shaken and the hills be removed,
yet my unfailing love for you will not be shaken
nor my covenant of peace be removed," says the Lord,
who has compassion on you.
Isaiah 54:10

Do not conform to the pattern of this world,
but be transformed by the renewing of your mind.
Then you will be able to test and approve what God's will is—
his good, pleasing and perfect will.
Romans 12:2

"This, then, is how you should pray: '
Our Father in heaven, hallowed be your name,
your kingdom come, your will be done, on earth as it is in heaven.
Give us today our daily bread. And forgive us our debts,
as we also have forgiven our debtors. And lead us not
into temptation, but deliver us from the evil one."
Matthew 6:9-13

*Yet it was the Lord's will to crush him and cause him to suffer,
and though the Lord makes his life an offering for sin...*
Isaiah 53:10

*"Father, if you are willing, take this cup from me;
yet not my will, but yours be done."
An angel from heaven appeared to him
and strengthened him. And being in anguish,
he prayed more earnestly,
and his sweat was like drops of blood
falling to the ground.*
Luke 22:42-44

The Lord longs to be gracious to you; he rises to show you compassion.
Isaiah 30:18

*For it has been granted to you on behalf of Christ
not only to believe in him, but also to suffer for him.*
Philippians 1:29

We must go through many hardships to enter the kingdom of God.
John 16:33

*My son, if you accept my words and store up my commands
within you, turning your ear to wisdom and applying your heart
to understanding—indeed, if you call out for insight and cry aloud
for understanding, and if you look for it as for silver and search for it
as for hidden treasure, then you will understand the fear
of the LORD and find the knowledge of God. For the LORD gives
wisdom; from his mouth come knowledge and understanding.*
Proverbs 2:1-6

*[John] sent his disciples to ask [Jesus], "Are you the one who is to
come, or should we expect someone else?"*
Matthew 11:2

Jesus replied, "Go back and report to John what you hear and see: The blind receive sight, the lame walk, those who have leprosy are cleansed, the deaf hear, the dead are raised, and the good news is proclaimed to the poor."
Matthew 11:4-5

Jesus said, "Truly I tell you, among those born of women there has not risen anyone greater than John the Baptist."
Matthew 11:11

For just as we share abundantly in the sufferings of Christ, so also our comfort abounds through Christ.
2 Corinthians 1:5

Answer me, Lord, out of the goodness of your love; in your great mercy turn to me.
Psalm 69:16

In this you greatly rejoice, though now for a little while you may have had to suffer grief in all kinds of trials. These have come so that your faith—of greater worth than gold, which perishes even though refined by fire— may be proved genuine and may result in praise, glory and honor when Jesus Christ is revealed.
1 Peter 1:6-7

Give thanks to him who made the heavenly lights— His faithful love endures forever. The sun to rule the day, His faithful love endures forever. And the moon and stars to rule the night. His faithful love endures forever.
Psalm 136:7-9 NLT

"I the Lord do not change."
Malachi 3:6

Your word is a lamp for my feet, a light on my path.
Psalm 119:105

For everything that was written in the past was written to teach us, so that through the endurance taught in the Scriptures and the encouragement they provide we might have hope.
Romans 15:4

I will sing to the Lord all my life;
I will sing praise to my God as long as I live.
Psalm 104:33

Now, my God, may your eyes be open and your ears attentive to the prayers offered in this place.
2 Chronicles 6:40

"For this reason a man will leave his father and mother and be united to his wife, and the two will become one flesh. So they are no longer two, but one flesh. Therefore what God has joined together, let no one separate."
Mark 10:7-9

Two are better than one, because they have a good return for their labor; If either of them falls down, one can help the other up. But pity anyone who falls and has no one to help them up. Also, if two lie down together, they will keep warm. But how can one keep warm alone? Though one may be overpowered, two can defend themselves. A cord of three strands is not quickly broken.
Ecclesiastes 4:9-12

Husbands, love your wives, just as Christ loved the church and gave himself up for her.
Ephesians 5:25

Trust in the Lord with all your heart
and lean not on your own understanding;
in all your ways submit to him,
and he will make your paths straight.
Proverbs 3:5-6

For you created my inmost being;
you knit me together in my mother's womb.
I praise you because I am fearfully and wonderfully made.
Psalm 139:13

So God created mankind in his own image,
in the image of God he created them;
male and female he created them.
Genesis 1:27

"For I know the plans I have for you," declares the Lord,
"plans to prosper you and not to harm you,
plans to give you hope and a future."
Jeremiah 29:11

He was despised and rejected by mankind, a man of suffering,
and familiar with pain. Like one from whom people hide their faces
he was despised, and we held him in low esteem. Surely he took up
our pain and bore our suffering, yet we considered him punished
by God, stricken by him, and afflicted. But he was pierced for our
transgressions, he was crushed for our iniquities; the punishment that
brought us peace was on him, and by his wounds we are healed.
Isaiah 53:3-5

This is how God showed his love among us: He sent his one
and only Son into the world that we might live through him.
This is love: not that we loved God, but that he loved us
and sent his Son as an atoning sacrifice for our sins.
1 John 4:9-10

Because of the Lord's great love we are not consumed,
for his compassions never fail. They are new every morning;
great is your faithfulness.

Lamentations 3:22-23

"Come to me, all you who are weary and burdened,
and I will give you rest. Take my yoke upon you and learn from me,
for I am gentle and humble in heart, and you will find rest
for your souls. For my yoke is easy and my burden is light."

Matthew 11:28

The Lord is the everlasting God, the Creator of the ends
of the earth. He will not grow tired or weary, and his understanding
no one can fathom. He gives strength to the weary and increases
the power of the weak. Even youths grow tired and weary,
and young men stumble and fall; but those who hope in the Lord
will renew their strength. They will soar on wings like eagles;
they will run and not grow weary, they will walk and not be faint.

Isaiah 40:28-31

"I have told you these things, so that in me you may have peace.
In this world you will have trouble. But take heart!
I have overcome the world."

John 16:33

He has delivered us from such a deadly peril, and he will deliver us.
On him we have set our hope that he will continue to deliver us.

2 Corinthians 1:10

But I will sing of your strength,
in the morning I will sing of your love;
for you are my fortress, my refuge in times of trouble.

Psalm 59:16

"Because he loves me," says the Lord, "I will rescue him; I will protect
him, for he acknowledges my name. He will call on me, and I will
answer him; I will be with him in trouble."
Psalm 91:15-16

Cast all your anxiety on him because he cares for you.
1 Peter 5:7

Let the morning bring me word of your unfailing love,
for I have put my trust in you. Show me the way I should go,
for to you I entrust my life.
Psalm 143:8

Let all that I am praise the Lord;
may I never forget the good things he does for me.
Psalm 103:2 NLT

Do not be anxious about anything, but in every situation, by prayer
and petition, with thanksgiving, present your requests to God. And
the peace of God, which transcends all understanding, will guard
your hearts and your minds in Christ Jesus.
Philippians 4:6-7

I waited patiently for the Lord; he turned to me and heard my cry.
He lifted me out of the slimy pit, out of the mud and mire;
he set my feet on a rock and gave me a firm place to stand.
He put a new song in my mouth, a hymn of praise to our God.
Many will see and fear the Lord and put their trust in him.
Psalm 40:1-3

The Lord does not look at the things people look at. People look at the
outward appearance, but the Lord looks at the heart.
1 Samuel 16:7

Peace I leave with you; my peace I give you. I do not give to you as the world gives. Do not let your hearts be troubled and do not be afraid.
John 14:27

*The Lord is close to the brokenhearted
and saves those who are crushed in spirit.*
Psalm 34:18

*Jesus said, "For I have come down from heaven
not to do my will but to do the will of him who sent me."*
John 6:38

*And they have defeated him by the blood of the Lamb
and by their testimony. And they did not love their lives so much
that they were afraid to die.*
Revelation 12:11 NLT

*Nevertheless, each person should live as a believer in whatever
situation the Lord has assigned to them, just as God has called them.*
1 Corinthians 7:17

*I have fought the good fight, I have finished the race,
I have kept the faith.*
2 Timothy 4:7

*Our days may come to seventy years, or eighty, if our strength endures;
yet the best of them are but trouble and sorrow,
for they quickly pass, and we fly away.*
Psalm 90:10

Hymns

A Collection of Public Domain Hymns
http://www.pdhymns.com

Leaning on the Everlasting Arms: Elisha A. Hoffman, 1887.
It Is Well: Horatio G. Spafford, C. Austin Miles, 1873.
He Leadeth Me: Joseph H. Gilmore, 1862.
I Love to Tell the Story: A. Katherine Hankey,
    William G. Fischer, 1866.
Wherever He Leads I'll Go: B.B. McKinney, 1936.
To God Be the Glory: Lyrics by Fanny Crosby, 1872.
Turn Your Eyes upon Jesus: Helen H. Lemmel, 1922.
'Tis So Sweet to Trust in Jesus: Louisa M. R. Stead, 1882.
I Need Thee Every Hour: Annie S. Hawks, Robert Lowry, 1872.
Trust and Obey: Lyrics by John H. Sammis, 1887.
Have Thine Own Way: Adelaide A. Pollard, 1907.
What a Friend We Have in Jesus: Joseph M. Scriven, 1855.
Rock of Ages: Augustus M. Toplady, Thomas Hastings. 1776.
How Firm a Foundation: Robert Keene, 1787.
Love Lifted Me: James Rowe, 1912.
Blessed Assurance: Fanny Crosby, 1873.
Standing on the Promises: R. Kelso Carter, 1866.
I Surrender All: Judson Van DeVenter, 1896.
Softly and Tenderly Jesus is Calling: Will L. Thompson, 1880.
We Are Standing on Holy Ground: Geron Davis, 1983.
How Great Thou Art: Carl Boberg,1886.
Amazing Grace: John Newton, 1779.
I'll Fly Away: Albert Brumley, 1929.

Notes

Chapter 1

[1] "I've Read the Last Page of the Bible!" *Billy Graham Life and Quotes WORLD CHRISTIAN NEWS RSS.* N.p., n.d. Web. 09 Feb. 2015.

Chapter 3

[2] *God's Purpose in Difficult Times* by Alan Redpath; Collection 238; [May 11, 2005]; Ephemera; 1958, 1961.

[3] Dunn, Bill, and Kathy Leonard. Through a Season of Grief: Devotions for Your Journey from Mourning to Joy. Nashville, TN: Nelson, 2004. Print.

Chapter 5

[4] Smiley, Captain Scotty. Decorated war veteran who lost his sight in combat. Author of the book *Hope Unseen.*

Chapter 6

[5] Sammons, Chris. Sermon notes. 11 Aug. 2013.

Chapter 7

[6] "Sound An Alarm." Sound An Alarm The Providence of God Part 3 Comments. N.p., n.d. Web. 14 Feb. 2015.

[7] Piper, John. "Desiring God." *Desiring God.* N.p., n.d. Web. 09 Feb. 2015.

[8] Hobbs, Brenda. Family Matters Bible Study. Oct. 2010.

Chapter 9

[9] "Broken Heart Syndrome." *Definition.* N.p., n.d. Web. mayoclinic.org.12 Feb. 2015.

[10] "The Sacredness of a Broken Heart." *Today's Christian Woman.* N.p., n.d. Web. 09 Feb. 2015.

[11] Whatchristianswanttoknow.com. Rick Warren on Brokenhearted, n.d. Web.

Chapter 10

[12] *Dictionary.com.* Dictionary.com, n.d. Web. 09 Feb. 2015.

[13] *Dictionary.com.* Dictionary.com, n.d. Web. 09 Feb. 2015.

Chapter 11

[14] Johns, Bob. 2 Feb. 2013.

[15] "Billy Graham." *Goodreads.* N.p., n.d. Web. 09 Feb. 2015.

[16] "Livingstone, David (1813-1873) - Gospel Fellowship Association." *Livingstone, David (1813-1873) - Gospel Fellowship Association.* N.p., n.d. Web. 09 Feb. 2015.

Chapter 12
[17] *People* Oct. 2013: n. pag. Web.

Chapter 13
[18] Janecka, Cindy. *Stars in the Darkness.* Jul. 2011.

Chapter 14
[19] Unknown.
[20] Hobbs, Brenda. Family Matters Bible Study.
[21] "Psalm 119 Matthew Henry's Commentary." *Psalm 119 Matthew Henry's Commentary.* N.p., n.d. Web. 09 Feb. 2015.

Chapter 15
[22] Lotz, Anne Graham. *Why?: Trusting God When You Don't Understand.* Nashville, TN: W Pub. Group, 2004. Print.

Chapter 16
[23] "A Quote by Charles R. Swindoll." *Goodreads.* N.p., n.d. Web. 09 Feb. 2015.
[24] Vassar, JR. Sondays Camp. Jul. 2012.

Chapter 17
[25] Guthrie, Nancy. Holding on to Hope: *A Pathway through Suffering to the Heart of God.* Wheaton, IL: Tyndale House, 2002. Print. Chuck Swindoll.

Chapter 18
[26] Vassar, JR. In a letter to his church, Apostle Church NYC, 9 Jun. 2013
[27] "Billy Graham." *Goodreads.* N.p., n.d. Web. 09 Feb. 2015.

Chapter 19
[28] Manser, Martin H. *The Westminster Collection of Christian Quotations.* Louisville: Westminster John Knox, 2001. Print. Corrie ten Boom.
[29] Hobbs, Brenda. Family Matters Bible Study. Jan. 2010.

Chapter 20
[30] Janecka, Cindy. *Mom's Prism of Love.* Nov. 2010.

Photo of Brenda Kay Keeton Hobbs

Courtesy of Tim Flanagan, Solas Gallery.

Back Cover

Photo by Colby Janecka.

Brenda Kay Keeton Hobbs

December 24, 1939 – December 1, 2010

I'll Fly Away

*I'll fly away, Oh Glory,
I'll fly away.
When I die, Hallelujah, by and by,
I'll fly away.*

Our days may come to seventy years,
or eighty, if our strength endures;
yet the best of them are but trouble and sorrow,
for they quickly pass, and we fly away.

Psalm 90:10